POETRY

FOR

PEOPLE:

FIFTY YEARS OF WRITING

by

DIXIE LUBIN

Independent Publishing

FOREWORD

Dixie Lubin, in her ecstatic poetry collection, *Poetry for People: Fifty Years of Writing*, asks at the end of one of her magical poems, 'Will you agree to stay and grow/ And heal this madly tilting world?' She has done just that in this in these deeply original, wildly embodied poems. Each poem engages with 'the landscape of time' not just in her one life but in what many of us experience in the kaleidoscopes of our lives, which she describes as 'Not just patterns/ But an infinite falling/ Into the country of love.'

We cannot help but fall into that country when we read these shimmering, surprising, and stunning poems, so many showing us how to live and love with greater abandon and imagination. Swirling together the likes of Kuan Yin, midlife crises, Thomas Merton, being a young girl in Kansas springtime, Ancient Corn Mother, cellos, and chickens, Dixie shows us the truth of the title of one of her many ecstatic poems: 'When you reach the bottom, go deeper!'

— Caryn Mirriam-Goldberg, Kansas Poet Laureate Emeritus

INTRODUCTION

Dixie Lubin has worn many hats in her extraordinary life— mother, partner, teacher, witch— but the one constant has been that of an artist. The publication of this volume represents the fulfillment of many lifelong dreams, not only those of Dixie but of the many people who have known and been touched by her work.

Decades-worth of journals, notebooks, and many stacks of random loose-leaf papers were excavated from Dixie's art studio with the help of her daughter and granddaughters, then packaged and mailed across the country to her other two daughters on the West coast. Several packages and a couple of visits later, there were enough poems collected to create a full book (or maybe two!)

The process of sorting, typing, and editing took nearly a year, with her daughters, grandson, and friends pitching to convert a lifetime of work into digital form. Several more months of collaborating, sorting, organizing, formatting, and putting love into every single detail of the book brought it all together into a beautifully packaged collection, with the cover art chosen by Dixie from her own portfolio. Big extra thanks to Michael Schepps for lending his publishing expertise to make this real and to Caryn Mirriam-Goldberg for contributing a beautiful foreword.

It is our privilege and honor to share this book with you. Dixie has shaped the lives of so many through her presence. We hope this book does as well.

— Jennifer, Terra, and Maya Lubin (her daughters)

Contents

IF I TOLD THE TRUTH

CALLING SPIRITS

I HAVE LIVED

STILL LIFE WITH HUSBAND AND CHICKENS

Five years into the journey, and I
Long since knew there was no
Happy ever after: waking to child's
Or rooster's cry into bleak
Rural dawns, the hungry wood stove
First in a series of bellies I must fill.

Those were hopeful times, though
My lovely babies filled my eyes and days
And there really was no time to ask:
"Where did my life go?"
Though sometimes I fluttered, caged bird,
Against my tiny orbit: house to barn,
Barn to mailbox.
Each day, I hoped, would bring no
Small new tragedy— scream of butchered rabbit
I must transform into dinner, ducks
Frozen to the ice with useless feet.
I prayed we would not fight, spewing venomous
Frustration while our elfin daughters cringed.

This day, the ashen sky was dense
With falling flakes of snow, while bare electric
Light bulb gave an almost holy light
To the warm shabby kitchen where I baked.

He was gone so long I'd almost forgotten him
Amidst the cinnamon and balls of dough,
When the door flew open, and there he stood.
His cheeks were blooming and he had a barred rock
Chicken under each arm. Steam rose from him, and
He wore his long-forgotten grin.
"These are the best layers," he said. "See, I've given
Them little leg bands so we'll know which ones they are.
These are the best layers— Sophie and Bertha!"

Five years into the journey, and suddenly I thought
It might be worth it.

On the one side, the pain, on the other
The way he looked with snow in his beard
The way he was radiant
Holding those chickens.

TWO CELLOS

It was a golden afternoon
South wind blew showers
Of yellow leaves
As summer opened into autumn
Inside, two cellos glowed at center stage
With burnished reds and oranges

With harpsichord tinkling in the background
The cellos commenced a stately dialog:
Point and counterpoint, their mellow voices
Full of emotions felt but not named
Pulled the tears from me like magnets.

Two minutes passed, or ten,
I was drowning in the beauty and sorrow
Summer opened into autumn
As the ancient music played
I thought of the people who had left me
Behind, here on earth
To still drink deeply of life's gorgeous, toxic cup

Now the cellos are joined
By a passionate violin
Black haired and brilliant, the
Young woman urges her fingers,
Her bow, to ever-ascending flights.
I am captured completely
My heart soaring in this glory
Born of the seventeenth century,
This beautiful music of humans
Gathering for peaceful acts of power.
Even now, in our fragmented days
And doubt-filled nights, as
The reality we've claimed
As our own
Morphs quickly into unknown territory

Some that are of my clan
Have gone ahead, scouting the way

They are pioneers, they are ancestors
They bless our lives from within,
Murmuring from inside our hearts
Making their presence known at crucial moments
And they still have the power to make us laugh.

In the museum courtyard
The two cellos end their conversation
And a resonant silence prevails.
And I say my personal goodbyes.
Blessing Jim, who has gone ahead
Into mystery: old reliable friend,
Brother-in-law, deep thinker,
Sagittarian rascal, unique human being –
And blessing equally those of us
Who still remain.

UNTITLED

My marriage was like the old coat in the closet that's
lasted for decades. It isn't stylish anymore, nor is it
clean. It bears the stains of childbirth, a litter of
puppies born on it, clumsily mended rips and tears
like frayed sleeves picked apart by angry arguments.

I don't like to be seen in it, but there is no way to
throw it away. The pockets are full of strange objects,
each stone and button and toy a different story, a sad
secret, a funny incident too raw to tell the kids, an
often clenched stone of anger,
the unresolved lint of years.

The lining is also secret... it smells wonderfully
of you and me, my darling, smoke and sex and essential oils.
It is lined with dark blue silk and on lonely cold nights I put
the coat around me. It is still the warmest thing I own,
and I stroke the lining again
and again, as memories and visions rise up of all we have
done and been to each other.

I finger the objects
like talismans, dreaming of what the future may hold,
seeing generations of grandchildren romping on the
coat, spread like a generous blanket on the cold
ground. This coat is not beautiful, not special—
yet it is so beautiful, so fraught with its burden of love and
angst and experience that it is priceless.

TORNADO

Some moments shine
Resplendent in memory like
A garnet pebble in the stream
Of gray rocks. In childhood, the
Deep magic hovering around a car my
Grandma told me to stay away from:
"Gypsies," she said but I saw a human finger
Inked in the air, protecting and warning!
My mother waking me from my wet bed with her sobbing
For people who had died
In a nearby Kansas tornado that night.
At Grandpa's farm, Vernon, the hired boy
And I racing in fear to the small earth cellar
Where the home-canned goods were stored, only
To see a copperhead on the downward steps!
"The tornado took only the barn roof... that time!

UNTITLED

All that short January day
Clouds vied with blue, first
The puffy whites thickening
Into herds, then wind and pure
Blue azure glowing with the power of the sun.
By four, the sky was gray haze
Stitched by skywriting
Skeins of geese— we wondered if going to KC
Was a wild goose chase?
Leaving town on a major artery
Lined with malls and factories, we passed
Two waifs, a boy and a girl, their pit bulls
On short leashes. Huge backpacks weighted them down
And they were shivering, the boy valiant,
Holding up his hot pink sign
To the indifferent stream of traffic.
Although it was too dark to read
I knew the proximal message
"Feed us, love us, rescue us..." My husband
Busy with driving, never saw them, never slowed
The long, long threads of traffic turned their lights on
So many thousands intent on their errands, hurling
Themselves along in the cold darkness.
A little snow left
And the sky now striated with heavy pregnant layers
Of gray and black, claiming the kingdom of air,
Pushing downward, crushing the early sunset
To a tattered pink ribbon shining low in the west.

MUSING, JUST MUSING

Getting old is not a tragedy
It is nature doing what has to be.
We are running low on good lives for the new
The up and coming, and their reality
To me is stunning, but not what I need.
Indeed, I am still strong
But my thinking goes wrong
The lyrics of my favorite song
Leave my brain fighting migraine
Then show up again at three A.M.
I am terrible with money, it's seriously not funny
For fifty plus years I did not need to fear
My husband always managed on the money we had
I cleaned and cooked and felt really glad
That he was captain of our life raft.
Nearly everyone agreed that I was arty
And a little bit daft. He fought sickness
For most of his life, and as his wife
I helped him a lot, and he helped me, seriously
We always had affinity for each other
We were lovers for infinity and raised three daughters
Strong, lovely, smart.
And they still do their part
And miss their dad, but are always glad
To help me keep living
They are kind and forgiving
As I slowly fall apart, they encourage my art.
If my last years are still ahead, I no longer cook
Nor bake the bread.
I want to walk the good red road, carrying my gift
The one I have always had, and always need to share
I was born to love!

THAT DAY, 1972

That day in San Francisco
Started out in fog and a crazy
Argument; somehow we fed the baby
Scraped up the money
To go forth into the city
Wearing our tattered finery.

We ate lunch in the marina, fat cat
Territory, with lavish
Art galleries, yachts in the water
And mile-long sandwiches from Guidi Brothers.
From there, drifting inevitably to
Golden Gate Park, the old electric saw player
Drawing us in, while baby Jennifer, enchanted
By toy sailboats, ran straight into the pond,
Came up spluttering and bawling.

Later, the Ukrainians were holding
A folk festival, all dressed in poofy white skirts
And embroidered blouses, the men in boots
Wide pants, funny hats. Suddenly
The Cockettes strutted in, a street theater group
With lipstick and beards, opening three-dimensional
Pantyhose capes to reveal sequined pubes, hairy
Legs in hot high heels.

A ship had come in just then
The park flooded with sailors still in uniform
The Ukrainians danced on an outdoor stage, while
On the grass sailors danced with Cockettes
Or anyone else... mind-blown tourists
Did not know where to look
And some scrawny stoned musicians
Suddenly appeared, began to croon
The same lyrics
Over and over and over.

"Whatever happens," they sang to whining
Electric guitar. "Whatever happens!"

And the electric saw still skirling, moaning
In the background. "Whatever Happens!"
While ecstatic hippies flung their bodies
Through space. "Whatever happens, it's alright
It's all right, what happens is alright!"

And the day spun with an energy
Wilder than happiness,
Giddier than wisdom.
Ravens wheeled and wafted
On eucalyptus winds
And whatever happened
For the rest of my life
Whatever happened would be alright.

OLD

One day I woke and could not
Do my day, it happened again
Body said no, not doing that right now
And pain made me listen... the beginning
Of old age creeps in.
Then one day you look in the mirror
The girl inside does not recognize that old face
Other days, the dance goes on, as always
Dance of breakfast, chores, music
Maybe a little afternoon delight... some parts
Still work just fine, if a little slower.
Dance of experience continuing unaffected, but now
The old songs bring tears; thoughts
Of the bright dead now lost to us
My home fires still burned though he coughed from the smoke
Still I have a lot to learn and
Where have my glasses gotten to?
With age comes acceptance, compassion and detachment
I am here more for others and
I do not fear death.

I AM FROM WICHITA

I am from Wichita, Riverview Street
From our tenant, Mr. Harris's daily fish,
Alive in a bucket in the hallway.
I am from Mrs. Bagwell's roses, stolen by me
And taking food to Ms. Laverentz, who
Died in dire poverty, leaving the proverbial
Mattress stuffed with cash.

I am from first Southern Baptist Church
Doctor Thorn's words a meaningless rain
Above my head while I drew on the church bulletin
Or soared out-of-body through the rose window...
I am from daily bible readings, nickels for verses remembered
I am from baptism at eight, my little girl's robe
Weighted so it won't float up in the lighted tank
High above the sanctuary

I am from the world, outside my house, where God the Father
No longer seemed to be spying on my every move
Where the sky and earth were alive with magic, and
Animals looked in my eyes with silent wisdom.
I am from the trees that I leaned against and climbed
The little creek with swimming snakes
I am from the faerie circle of mushrooms
In my yard... I am from the mystery.

UNTITLED

Now is the time for composting
The enormous piles of experience
Tossing them in with manure and no attachment.
Turning them with the rake of skillful means
Waiting prayerfully for them to transition.
Now is the time to become
Part of the ground of being
Waiting, willing, accepting all comers—
The earthworms and the pill bugs
Raccoons and opossums, curious cats
Now is the time to use your old life
To nurture the new, the seeds
The up and coming... now is the time
To swoon with the strange beauty
Of the new, vibrant beings
Springing up everywhere.

EVOLVING

What I had was youth, curiosity, passion, burning
enthusiasm— the thrill of my path ahead, life was
mostly ahead of me.

What I lost, what I lost, was a true sense of myself. I
became entwined in relationships and forests of
relationship until I lost the vision of who I was, or
why...

What I am beginning is standing on the threshold
of old age, of looking and staring death in the face, of
opening my heart past what I thought was possible.

What I hope but do not know is the hope for
reincarnation... yes, I would come back to this
incredible, beautiful wild and wicked world, and would
choose to keep evolving.

A FEW MONTHS BEFORE THE VIRUS

I was driving in the city
My eyes seeking organic forms
The sinuous shapes of trees
Breaking the monotonous rectangles of buildings
And mown lawns. When there is a pause
In the endless cacophony of white noise vehicles
I sometimes hear crows calling one another
In their harsh language that my heart needs to hear.
When the tension of urban life
Grows to headache level
I find a place with water
Even the trickling rock in the Japanese garden
Relaxes my jaw and releases me from commercial
Messages bombarding..."Buy me, buy me, bye me"
I smile at my empty pockets
So unsuited for life in the city
I renounce attachment to Starbucks
And Cupcake Construction Company
Lie quietly in the park, carefree as a homeless drunk
With a whole bottle of wine...I only look up
Through fiery motes of sun that shine anywhere,
Without preference and release my angst...
The clouds! The clouds!

WINTER SOLSTICE 2016

Early, icy
Trudging out to scrape the windshield
Performing the ever more complex dance
Of staying on earth, it's slippery underfoot...
But the eastern sky runs through its changes
Reds and pinks like stained glass
Through the bare branches, clouds
Drift and roil.
He huffs his way to the van, stubborn old man
And I bless him for it...
I am in the driver's seat, even though yesterday
I backed into a power and light truck
Shattering a tail light, and my fragile grasp
On something I can't name. Our day will be difficult
As the one before, winter holidays striding
Toward us without mercy, everywhere
There are tidings of darkness and fear
Barely frosted over with tinsel and a scrim
Of Christmas carols... we are small creatures
Maintaining our bubble of warmth and breath
Striving, desperate, getting out the Menorah
Happy as field mice just to be alive.

UNTITLED

I can't wait for winter holidays
To come and go... nowadays they carry
Too much weight
The joys and sorrows
Of past years
The fears of what may be coming
Christmas carols on the radio
Still bring this old pagan to tears
I get back under the comforter
Joints aching fiercely— just before sleeping
My closed eyes see a flash of vivid green
Reminds me that spring too will return
The Goddess will return.

HISTORY REPEATS ITSELF

History repeats itself...
Same old story, guts and glory
Garbage on the shore
Forests no more— humans don't learn fast
Far too many animals have had to breathe their last
You might ask, isn't this new?
And I have to say no, not really
How many civilizations were based on peace
And conservation? How many did not make war
Or hunt and gather for more, more, more?
How many treated all spices as equal and teachers?
The Native Americans take the honors here!
But the past has always been brutal
For all its gifts — the present is intense
Misery so dense it's pollution
Will the future really bring for a good outcome?
I won't be holding my breath—
History repeats itself.

WE WERE POOR

We were poor
We had a garden
He had his ideas and
I had mine.
His rows were straight,
And I had chaotic beds
He planted vegetables
And expected me to work
Exactly as he did
I planted herbs
For wisdom, tea, and solace.
Basil every year
Biennial parsley
Mints and comfrey
Mother-of-thyme
Sage and mugwort
For smudging
Artemisia because
My friend liked to
Bury her nose
In it, and declare
It was the pubic hair of the goddess.

TALE FROM THE NINETIES

Young man in my living room
Slumped in Aunt Fifi's chair
Like a weary, wingless angel
Green gaze focused in the middle distance
His once brown hair
Now layered black on blond
Fresh from NYC, black jeans silk screened
Rubbed with bronze powder
Bright red nails set off his immaculate
White fingers.
His soft talk is of drugs remembered
And drugs anticipated
He pulls our dog's ears
And drinks my sodas.
Why is he here? It is not easy, but I care for him.
Once he was my daughter's friend... a character
A flamer... someone to tell stories about
That was, before he walked down the street
In full glorious drag and was beaten senseless
(Senseless beating!) by a drunken redneck
I visited him in hospital
Read his cards, tried to focus on the positive
That emerged like rocks from a river of despair
Seven years later he returned to his hometown.
Addicted, bipolar, applying for disability
He's come here looking for healing
Or just a place to stay
I think about how we are all connected
Like it or not, Rich is a part of me, I am a part
Of him. I think about how he has Buddha nature
How the walls that divide us
Are just an illusion.

UNTITLED

I was in my mama's belly
In rural Oregon, looking towards Mt. Hood
Being Kansas people, my parents moved to Wichita
Where I was born in bed
While the grandfather clock
Struck the midnight hour.
Wichita was my cradle
From my crazy first neighborhood
Just a block from the river
To a red brick Victorian on the other end of town.

By mid-teens, I couldn't wait to leave
I had been to Lawrence
It was where I wanted to be
Lawrence was my play house
Late adolescence, freedom
Music, boys, art, psychedelics
Midnight picnics, bottles of wine
Whoops— I forgot to go to class again.

Still restless, I journeyed to San Francisco
Just in time for the Death of Hippie parade down Haight Street
No money, bounced back to Kansas
Wichita to Lawrence (flunked out again) to Kansas City
Back to San Francisco
It was fun, like home
Later to NYC, then Paris
Then one country after another
I could have stayed in Italy
The boys there didn't mind if I was fat
I could have stayed in Turkey
But I had to get away from the opium.

SAD POEM 2016

It's all blue in our kitchen.
It's been a too bright teal
Contrasting with a dim pink
Since the early '90s,
Which drove our eldest crazy
When we chose it –
"It's so 80s, guys," she would say.

But that blue
Had gotten us through,
With me still cooking.

It's all blue in our house these days.
Not the pot smoke
Or the thin cloud of the vaporizer.
Yes, there's dust
But it is gray and immortal
This blue
Is emotion, too much feeling
Hanging in shreds
In every interchange

Pushing against my eyes
From the inside
Hanging in invisible clouds
From the walker, the wheelchair
The oxygen equipment
The boxes of medical supplies
Too much has gone wrong
Overnight we got old

My husband spends days in bed
TV remote at hand
He's up all night
Rocking and davening
Not really praying
Just keeping himself alive.

A DAY IN TEN PARTS

One

Has to be somewhere
Why not in the newborn light
Cascading through my east window
Crossing the bedroom at the speed of itself
Knocking, gentle and persistent, on
Closed doors of my eyelids?

Two

Two cups of too strong coffee
Too much diet sugar
Two too many pieces of toast
To calm the ravenous beast inside
You are too much, beast,
You win again.

Three

Three remarks have cut me
Before I make it out the door
One each dismissive, disrespectful, distrustful
Three times I bite down on sharp retorts
After all this time, I know they get me nowhere.

Four

Four starlings fly and frolic
Moving as one to the banquet of muffin crumbs
I have left on the table near the small pine
Four times black feathers flash
Iridescent in the sun.

Five

Five minutes to cross the bridge
In rush hour traffic
Through the open window, I turn
To the long body of the river
I am pulled into a dream
Floating to a different life
Maybe fifteen hundred miles from here
Maybe only five.

Six

Six ingredients make my dinner
I am fortunate indeed
Brown eggs from my sister's farm
Whipped to a frenzy
Slices of Yukon gold sautéed in the pan
With onion and red pepper.
Next, succulent greens spears from the garden
Last the salty crumbly goat cheese layers in
Finally, the eggs, in my grandma's cast iron skillet
Frittata!

Seven

Seven o'clock, and it's not hot
Or cold, on the sidewalk outside the coffee house
Where I sit with a shot of caffeine
Golden evening light is kind
To my friend's aging face and to mine.
Forty-five years we have talked
Never running out of things to say
And more important, things to laugh at.
I look at her and wonder
How many more years do we have?

Eight

Eight times a year, earth's energy shifts
As the season upon us freezes or sizzles
Crops are sown and reaped
Equinoxes balance light and dark
Solstices mark longest and shortest days
Between the arms of this medicine wheel
Lie the cross-quarter days, heralding
More subtle shifts
Times when the veil between realities
Grows thin – time to call the spirits, and invite them in.

Nine

Returning home at nine o'clock
We lock ourselves in, close the blinds, hold the old dog close
Listen to the public radio blues until midnight.

Ten

I used to sing 'Ten Little Indians,' and count on
My fingers and toes
Now I have asked you ten times to calm
Down, and lower your voice, but you
Have not been attentive, you've been on tenterhooks
You are very, very tense.
For my part, I am feeling
Tenuous; you are way too intense
I certainly don't want to dance attendance!
Still a tendril creeps from my heart to yours
And a bud of tenderness opens.

UNTITLED

Scary little spirits
Coming through the windows
Of the closed, locked, blacked-out
Ballet studio
Tiny lights flitting
A sigh of wind in the empty tight space
And then, closing around our sacred circle,
Touching (hard) our upraised hands.
We were only seventeen,
We ran like frightened hounds.

HARD WINTER

Such a hard winter it was
I felt reduced and closed away,
My house like a loose shell around me,
Wandering disconsolate from room to room,
Seeking unsuccessfully to suck at the media tit.
My bones were dry, heart aching, breathing difficult.
Pinched and grudging, I met the cold days with effort
And grinding gray fatigue.

Now it is spring
And branching neurons sprout
Tight hard buds of hope— will I blossom again
Before I tire of moonlight?
Will I bear a new harvest
Now that the children have grown and gone?

I fill the chalice on my altar
With clean, bright water,
Call to the Thunderbeings surely gathering in the west
With my hissing rainstick.
Beating my drum, I arouse the cosmos,
Announcing again and again
"I am here, send water."
My thirsty taste buds need tender mercy
To open their scented beauty
To the sky.

UNTITLED

This prairie dirt is rich with bones and stories
Step outside on winter nights and
Hear the spirit whispers carried on the wind.

Those who came before us, their lost voices
A chorus
Of pride and grief and joy.

Before the little empty towns
The desolate windswept farms
Before the smallpox took its toll and
The wagons rolled over the ground
There were those who walked so lightly,
Taking only what they needed.

People of the South Wind
Red and brown like Kansas earth
Danced the circle of the Year,
Accepting life and death and birth.

They fell as we will fall
The Mother took them in
This prairie dirt is red with blood and stories—
No beginning and no end.

WEDNESDAY AT WOUND CARE

On Wednesdays past
I drove my husband to wound care
I would sit in the waiting room where
The magazines never change, and were inane
In the first place... the patients appear
In ones or twos, mostly in wheelchairs
Most are elderly. Fred still walked in
Wearing his special boots we ordered on Amazon
For the days when his feet balloon past any shoes
I began to recognize faces and it slowly dawns on me
That for most of these patient patients, their
Wounds don't truly heal
Not really, not for long.
Swollen limbs full of fluid
Any bump can open like a fountain.
The nurses run the debridement, the meds,
The special pads and tightly wrapped up legs
Are all just slowing down the inevitable
And tears leave my eyes for his suffering
For everyone's suffering, because everyone here
Is suffering. Death is seldom beautiful
But it can be compassionate.
He was truly loved.

LAMPSHADES

Living in San Francisco
in 1967 I had no money to speak of.
Six of us shared a rickety little house in a
back alley in the Mission. I wanted to make
art, but had no money for canvas, gesso, etc.
So I thought 'what CAN I paint?'

At the Salvation Army and other thrift stores often
there were old silk lampshades, white or
neutral beiges for one or two dollars apiece.
I had inherited a set of industrial strength, permanent
black markers from an itinerant speed freak, and I would
Buy those lampshades and decorate them, sort of like
Tiffany lamps, with lots of elegant black outlines and
jewel-tone colors, but mixed in with the flowers and
butterflies and grapevines were: eyes, copulating figures, radiant
    Buddhas,
beetles, junkyards, machinery— the flotsam and jetsam of my
    consciousness.

When they were put on lamps and light
shone through them, they were a psych-a-delic
wonderland! (Especially after a couple of tokes.)
From lampshades I went on to decorating men's underwear (new!),
the same sort of style with lots of demure maidens peeking out of
    grottoes,
opium dreams, dragons, and gigantic phallic cacti!

WITHOUT MY HUSBAND

Sometimes my day is locked, feels
Like just your house, its small menaces
Walls, floors... a comfort zone
Or maybe even there
In your empty marriage bed you wrestle
With biting ants, brown spiders, your own
Demons. On days like this, Facebook palls
And you can't find your email any more
You look in your mailbox for signs
From the universe
Then maybe you will see a red-tailed hawk
Or just the robin babies under the hedge.
Other days open wide
Walking on the ground you commune
With the life force, vibrating you in the force field
The hum that keeps weaving you
Back into your life, goes on to fill your heart
With the greatness of creation
Driving through eastern Kansas
Filling your eyes with trees and vistas
Small photogenic towns, black cows,
A good coffee shop?
Every possibility opens to usher you
With the assurance that the path unfolds
Just before your feet.

LOVE OF THE PAST

Memories of marvels— the trembling awareness
Of the baby girl, my magic childhood a talisman
I carry in my heart, when life stretched ahead like open seas.
Cold water from my rural grandmother's metal dipper
Smell and sight of kerosene lanterns at dusk
So small I was, I understood everything
Wordless at the magnificence of night sky
Aware that the moon followed me everywhere.

Love of the past
A curious girl's horizons
That first passionate kiss, and the silky unexpected spill
His semen in my wondering hand
Diana Sue Brooks' wondrous breasts
The way we taught crows at the Wichita Zoo to swear on command.

Love of the past, young adult becoming
Liberated from past hang-ups
Thanks to powerful psychedelics I experienced.
My body breaking into dancing energy patterns
Knowing there was no me, then me again.
Images rushing from my hands, journeys,
Babies coming through and filling my life
Learning— so hard— to pay attention.

Love of the past, painful, wonderful human love
Simple love, complicated love, lover love, lust love
Man love, woman love
Dance of experience continuing in wonder.
Taking psilocybin and going to the corner store
I met God in person
She was a little black girl
About eight years old.
The whole history of the Universe, known and unknown
Danced in her eyes— I wanted to bow down
But the Vietnamese grocery man looked like a grumpy demon
So I left to continue my journey.

Love of the journey
Love of always going on
Learning love of the difficult
And how it teaches me.
Love of new horizons
When I can't travel in this body
Any longer, I'll go inside myself
And learn to send my spirit
To the corners of the Universe.

UNTITLED

First thing I really noticed
Was the energy of the earth,
The elements humming and sparking
For me as a child, the thread of magic!
Roses beckoned me
To pick them, the eyes of the neighbor's cat
Seeming to know me—

Lying on my back in
Tickling grass, the sky
Never stopped changing.
Signs written in the air,
Leaves and dirt essential.
Fire a big bright mystery,
Exciting and dangerous
Water most of all
Fountaining in downtown Wichita
Or streaming by
My Grandpa's farm
With a snake undulating by—

I felt the Divine everywhere outdoors
Not so much in Baptist Church
Weather was something
To embrace each day
Loving the lightning
Heat and snow, and the wind
Whispered to me of its journey—

School and church playmates
Came and went
But I felt the loom of
Causality wearing me
I felt bliss and joyous
Sexual stirrings
Life was a whole-body orgasm
And the thread was elemental joy.

GIRL INTO WOMAN

I came to you in the time of my first flowering.
Not furled stem or hard green but, I was
Fully open, fragrant, petals quivering with desire.
This rapid, tumbling world is one of change,
But ancient stories still repeat, as seed unfolds
Into green, growing plant.
The real and mythical maiden that I was
Rushes all unconscious toward that state of grace
And suffering known as Mother.

Even then I was no slender waif
The full unblemished moon of my belly
Glowed faintly in the dark with the nacreous
Luster of healthy skin. Globes of breast
And buttock, generous curve of thigh
All bespoke the deep feminine, the earth-mother joy
Of opening wide like a blossom
To receive the seeds of my future children.

I loved you without ideas or reservations
As a flower turns to the sun, and
Looking at old photographs, I see with detachment
Of hindsight that I was beautiful; the glossy,
Passionate vitality of the untempered young.
I could not refuse you my mouth, my body in
Constant readiness for your most thoughtless caress.
As a flower bravely opens, revealing her innermost heart,
Her innocent sexuality
Poignant and delicate as music, so I gifted you
With my vulnerability— you were my sun,
My buzzing bee— I nodded and bent
In the changing winds of your regard.

This headlong, rapid world is not kind to flowers.
You were drawn to me naturally
Yet culture dictated that my well-upholstered curves
Were outside the parameters of desire.
Struggling with your own evolution

You were cruel, you told me not to stay
Unless I changed my form to suit the norm.
By then, spring had changed to summer.
Inevitably, I quickened
Growing heavier with child.
Ancient stories repeat themselves.

As flower slowly swells to fruit,
I ripened. The mother is sweet, juicy fruit
Offering her essence to nourish others.
Unflinching, I fed my green and growing daughters.
As they become maidens, my mother-self becomes crone.
Stripped to my essence, seed again, hard and furrowed
With a bitter kernel of wisdom deep inside.
Strange how the seed contains, genetically encoded,
The entire cycle of life.

I came to you in my first flowering.
Young yourself, you were not aware
Of the greatness of that gift.
Yet you did not leave me
And now we grow old, learn to honor
Pain as well as joy. If we have not loved well,
We have endured, with the stubborn pride
Of all survivors.
Leaning together, alternately squabbling and cooing,
We shelter each other from the cold wind, and wait.

MY FUTURE DANCE

Still here at home
Not much urge to roam
House full of memory
Not exactly haunting me but
It's a bit daunting
My ghost, my departed love
Has not fully left
After 53 years together
We are both bereft.

And everywhere I look
There are shelves full of books
The ones, among others
That he hoped to read
But did not succeed
I had different tastes
But don't want the books to go
I think of him, sometimes
Every day or so.

When I watch drama on TV
I often start to weep
Or maybe I won't sleep
I need an anti-sadness book
With instructions
On my future dance
How to be bold in your
Creaking house alone
Hoping I will get up on time
Calls on our old phone.

Finding folks to do the mowing
Ask the grandkids to help
With the garden sowing
The house and yard together
In every kind of weather
Is too much for one old woman.

FLAMBOYANT

Rich went downtown Lawrence on a Friday night
Dressed like a girl, and he looked alright
His hair was long, his makeup well done,
A sexy dress and fishnets to impress.

High platform heels and he could do the walk
A young man like many, just wanting to talk,
To connect, have some drinks at the bar
Find some action with a man of his choice.
This was Lawrence in the nineties.

He knew the Replay Lounge
Would let him in—
He was beautiful!
He was flamboyant.

But in the alley after midnight
No date had materialized.
Drunk and angry men, uglier
Than Rich could ever be
Sent him to the hospital, broken
In mind and body.

Tell me again which ones are the "bad guys?"

I HAVE LIVED

I have lived— midcentury, midwest, middle class
girl fed on eggs and bacon,
beef for dinner, Jello for dessert.
Fed the story of Jesus
for spiritual sustenance,
daily Bible readings,
enforced Saturday evenings at Youth for Christ.

I have lived— as a young beatnik surrealist
artist and poet, reciting Zen poems while standing
in the trash basket at Wichita North High, while
girls primped in mirrors, trying to ignore me.
I dragged a briefcase in the halls all day
on a ten-foot rope, drank
secret whiskey and practiced
with a bullwhip.

I have lived— burgeoning hippie, marching for civil rights,
women's rights, making my poems,
discussing existentialism in seedy coffeehouses,
in communes where everyone floated
in a sea of hormones, dope, great music
and revolution.
The neighbors knocked on my commune door
to borrow a cup of dope and the next day when
we showed up at their door naked under our coats,
they sheepishly stripped to underwear
and served us killer brownies.

I have lived— in San Francisco, twice,
made soup with the Diggers, danced to
Jefferson Airplane in Golden Gate Park with our toddler,
and accidentally took a speed freak home to dinner.
I took speed myself and saw every fish in the aquarium
in forty-five minutes.

I have loved— men and women,
borne children, been a welfare Mom married

to a man with breathing problems,
worked for the IRS on the midnight shift,
until one night I fainted and was informed by my body
that I was pregnant.
I have been— a teacher and a nanny, and always,
always! written and made art, no matter what.
I sold brooms made by blind people, worked in an office
wearing pantyhose and my disdain.
I've battled compulsive eating and bad genes.
I have kissed the feet of a guru and done pagan magic
That did not fail its purposes.

I have lived—and I will keep living, opening
To all of it, opening my heart
and saying, "Yes!"

MY CHOSEN LANDSCAPE

REMEMBERING

That early February day
When the sun
Toasted everything, when
Snowdrops raised their questions
And we went to the lake... leaving the van
My breath flowed freely, and the light
So harsh in town seemed to caress me
As it filtered through stalwart cedars.

I limped down the hill with my cane
The natural floor welcomed my feet
Last year's weeds clung to me, asking me
Mutely
To pick up the trash.

I reached the place where the trees were
Speaking
And bowing with the wind
Where my heart opened.

I bloomed greenly with the full, rich
Love of the trees, of the lake filled with wavelets
All of the love pouring
In and out of me... in those quiet moments
I walked around the gateless gate
And fell into the arms of the universe.

UNTITLED

Let the mystery of twilight
Pervade your senses step by
Slow step while the breeze
Rustles green bountiful leaves
Let the aroma of honeysuckle
Enchant nostrils tired of urban smells
As the sun departs in a fanfare of color
Let the rush-hour street sounds fade
As sparrows return to rustling bamboo
And the ink of night begins to stain the air
Let tensions of the day relax into
The limbo of the past, as clouds
Grow purple in the West.
Let televisions and computers go on buzzing
In a million houses
While outside the world breathes benediction
Let your soul rest secure in this webbed moment
When you are connected: to moon rising
To grass between toes
To the whip-poor-will's sweet cry.

A MORNING IN THE FLINT HILLS

Earth speaks silently,
as the Plains unroll outside
the car window, in or out

Earth speaks powerfully,
her heartbeat synch became like mine with
her hot magma at the core, plates restlessly shifting
past passion powering me, past pain and fear,
past my uneasy squirming at the steady state
of reality

Earth speaks with utmost compassion,
choosing to foster every creature,
giving all a fair chance to grow or fail or
start again, when sadness becomes
unbearable, when there is no one to turn to

I throw myself upon her green grass, her brown body,
give her my anguish, feed her with cornmeal
and tears, feel my sorrow without words, She
takes the worst of it, recycles, reuses

The earth speaks in the voices of trees,
screaming as they fall, in the eyes of infant gorillas,
the sunrise of birds

She is my true mother, I can't
live one day without her!
She is calling more loudly each day and
I cannot live one day without her
Yes— it is your turn, to help me if you can.

THE HINGE ON THE DOOR

Between winter and spring
Creaks open, in dim darkness
Before dawn... Crocus longing
For the light, leave earthy soil behind
As they thrust their green spears upward
Praising the rising sun.

FROM THE COLUMBIA GORGE

It's so easy to fall in love with rivers
Those natural companions of the road
Whose very names are the stuff of stories:
Columbia, Clearwater, and Snake,
Little Bighorn, Yellowstone, Powder.

I love the way they curl through landscape
With effortless feng shui... the serpentine energy
Of dragons at play. Rivers rush headlong, like reality
Never stopping, always changing; now broad and serene
A mighty flow, but before complacency sets in
There's turbulence: narrows, rocks, and rapids
Forks and creeks, cascades, waterfalls, and always
The song water sings, primeval, profound, this ancient
Music will lull you to infant slumber at night
Greet you at sunrise with cheerful energy.

Siddhartha sat listening to the voice of the river
Until he filled with light. All stories are there,
From the first raindrop to the carving of great gorges
Your great grandmother's voice, the wailing of lost tribes.
Ask a foolish question: Are you dangerous? How many fish?
Where do you begin and end? And river will chuckle
Endlessly 'til questions fall away, and there is only birdsong,
Cloud mind, diamond light on water, rainbow spray.

OCTOBER

October, gathering gold and orange leaves
Blue wind spiraling them into patterns
That fall to damp ground
Where butterflies drink
Inviting sun through windows
Shining onto polished tables
Or spilling onto sheets
Tousled by afternoon delights.

October, geese gathering overhead
Filling sky with bird calligraphy— messages
Unreadable but filled with mystery and longing.
Rainclouds gathering, sky darkening
Sudden chill, drops on wet bamboo
Puddles cold on still bare feet.

October, Persephone gone underground
The trees begin to drop their garments
As Demeter walks weeping, inconsolable
The small graceful aspen shimmies, shimmers
Drops her leaves like a slow-motion strip tease.
The catalpa hurls its leaves to the ground
With a vengeance. Maples linger, making love
To the sun as long as possible.

October nights chill and lengthen
A certain sadness hangs like mist.
The ancestors hover, coming closer
Hoping to be honored while the veil between the worlds
Is thin.

October gathers us in to ourselves
Going deep and quiet
Remembering, reflecting
Drawing in our parameters
Under our quilts at night
Stars and galaxies gather out the window
And we hope for dreams
To sustain us through the cold.

MELON

It's the third huge watermelon this month
Not a small one for two
Or a decent-sized family melon.
This one feels heavy as a cannon
And carrying it, you visualize dropping,
Seeing in your mind
The cracked pink disaster
Crying juices everywhere.

Even if you get it to the sink
To wash, and haul it to the table
Get out your cleaver
And hack it into half.
Half won't fit into the fridge.
Too much melon, I say,
Why this again?
I urge the girls to eat until they're stuffed.

I fill up gallon bags
With red chunks
And freeze them,
There is sticky juice everywhere
My own belly aches
With the load of watermelon
Entering my mouth,
August in Kansas.

ANCIENT CORN MOTHER

Ancient Corn Mother, come to me
Make my way sacred
Fill me with beauty
That I may bring others beauty
Corn Mother cannot really die
All these old ones are immortal
As long as humans pass stories
Down the generations
But the ceremonies are nearly forgotten
The young only know the empty pleasures
Of the dominant paradigm
All the corn on the planet
Even Inca corn in the Andes
Is genetically contaminated
Monsanto strides the world
Grabbing all the seeds and owning them, changing them
Corn Mother never knew
Her magnificent gift to so many creatures
Would be conscripted, twisted and abused
Corn Mother waits, listening— imaging the
Sacred chants, watching, hoping
To see the dancers on the hot dusty plaza
Once again... waits and watches
Heart longing for the beauty of the dancing
Corn Maidens, watches
For the designs the medicine men make
From the holy pollen....
The design is ruined, kicked aside
The people grope in darkness
Where has our sacred universe gone?

MY CHOSEN LANDSCAPE

If I could choose
A time, a place, a season
Beyond reason— a magic land
In which to stand.
It could be here and now
Or maybe here and then...
Imagine Eastern Kansas one hundred years ago
Or in some vastly unknown future.
I know there would be more birds
More trees, less words
I see the Flint Hills
Vast seas of green
Bison herds and small holdings
Villages with sun power, wind power.
Empowered people
Powerful children
Playing music, working and playing
Under a clear, endless sky.

UNTITLED

Always the sky
Meets the ground.
Wherever you go
The horizon recedes,
Beckoning.
As you leave the prairie
The mountain ranges of your future
Look like clouds
Or the far clouds
Look like mountains.
Soon enough
You will be among them
Looking down
On your valley life
So small, possibly pointless
All your heroic efforts
Antlike, scurrying, futile
As you see the shadow...
Death foot rising
And coming down hard.

THIS UNIVERSE

This Universe of ours
So mysterious...
Scientists never cease
To investigate our planet,
Find out all that humans can.
Gorgeous sisters, magnificent brothers—
Most of us try to be good
In our own way.

Most of us fumble and fall
Most of us hit the wall, we hope
To once again be a part of it all.
We drop thirty pounds
And lose our wedding rings
Or we join up in a choir; we'd always hoped to sing
And meet a promising guy or gal.

Ready or not, Everything
Is so beautiful
Until it isn't, but we just keep soaking it,
Soaking it in!
This Universe of ours.

UNTITLED

Be still and know
That you will not regret
The remarks that would otherwise
Escape your loose lips
Be still and learn
That you can become invisible
In any crowd
Observing human behavior
At your leisure
Be still on the earth
Let Her sing
Songs of water and tree
Birdsong and sighing wind
Allow Her strength to comfort you
Don't be surprised by your tears
Offer them silently
Be still when you are angry
Feel the blue veins throbbing
The infernal heat of your face
Listen to your own inner voice
Become passionate in defense
Of your indubitably correct position!
Let it subside without comment
Be still with a newborn baby, any species
Holding securely
Letting your breathing harmonize
With his or hers
Put the downy head near your chest
Your heartbeat will flood him
With love and welcoming
Songs can wait a week or so!

IN SPITE OF EVERYTHING

In spite of everything, THE MOON.
Serene above my nightly worries glows
And shows perhaps her fullest Buddha face
Or, newly minted, twinkles
A modest silver fingernail.

This stately lunar entity
That pulls the tides must pull on me
Forty years asked monthly
For my tears and woman's blood
And still she calls to my wild coyote heart
So I must find my pack of friends and howl
Or hooting, imitate the owl.

In spite of everything, the foolish choices
And the rocky roads, the lost worlds
Hurling through vast interior spaces
Like orphaned planets
In spite of sad brave jokes and downright failure
Gratuitous human cruelty and those moments
Of raw beauty nearly as devastating
That Moon floats above it all, keeps
Her schedule, a promise I can count on.

One night she's gone
Sky seems desolate, a jilted lover
Darkly brooding
It is then I go inside myself
Search my heart for lumps of treasure
Of the passing days, then close the curtains
Of my eyes, and sleep— so deep, so deep
So dreaming deep.

When she returns, like a cosmic wink
In firmament of spangled ink
I kiss my hand to her
And feel new energies stir and rise
It's time for new beginnings
I'm young again, yet strangely wise.

Then it is, she opens me
A starfish in a vibrant, cleansing tide
Red heart beating between my legs
In ancient cadence
While mad songs flutter my brain
Gray moths at the window.

I think I may go crazy then
Unless I drop the clothes of care
And run to enter still, dark water
Or go naked to some fragrant, night blooming garden
Where I may praise her ancient ways and say
"In spite of everything, THE MOON!"

OUR SNAKY SISTERS

Scaled and sensuous
Listening with their bellies
To the songs of earth.
Drinking the milk of priestesses
In initiation caves
Whispering to slinky seers with
Sighing syllables, our snaky sisters
Were once held in honor

Sacred pythons
Predict earthquakes
By climbing straight up

Dancing cobras
Exotically swaying
To throbbing atonal flute music

Rainbow boas large as myth
And so lovely
Winding their way
Through dreaming rain forest
Slithering into the compounds
Of medicine men
Drunk on vision vine with
Stoned Americans
And take them on the snake eyes tour
Of the jungle!

All respected, all sacred
Seen perhaps with fear
But acknowledged for their beauty

My mother was from Arkansas backwoods
She was 14 when the old Cottonmouth
Bit her in the creek
Her mother soaked it in kerosene, her only medicine
And mom lived to tell the tale
To her, snakes were near to the devil!

In the dawn of time
A priestess trots through stinging hot desert
Her woven basket full
Of poisonous snakes
All of them her friends
All healers if you know their secrets
She has been gladly bitten
Again and again
So she can transmute their venom
Into healing

GAIA

Gaia's so gorgeous
Wearing Her harvest gown
A sea of vibrant greens
Watered by Her tears
Flowers embroidered randomly
Along Her broad flanks
Glints of gold in fields not yet reaped
In spite of all that's happened
The indignities She bears
In fraught silence or terrible storms
Her beloved species destroyed without mercy
Her crops mutating (you know She's angry
When five volcanoes erupt simultaneously)
In spite of the heartless way we cover her,
With roads and poison cities
She knows She will prevail... humans are too clever
By half, they merrily engineer their own destruction
Yes, She will miss our songs as much as
She will miss the birds. Still, Her harvest garb
Is splendid, She wears the best perfumes:
Rosemary, lemon balm, basil and sage
She's survived so many catastrophes
And knows She will endure. If humans go, oh
When humans go, Her grains and grasses will abound
She will wait with unearthly patience.

NOVEMBER

Persephone gone underground
The trees began to drop their garments
As Demeter walks, weeping, inconsolable
The small graceful aspen shimmies, shimmers
She drops her leaves like a slow-motion striptease
The catalpa in my yard hurls its heart-shaped leaves
With a vengeance
Maples linger, making bright
Love to the sun, as long as possible
November nights chill and shorten, a sadness hangs like mist
The ancestors hover, coming closer
Hoping to be honored
While the veil between worlds is thin

EGG

It must have come first.
After all, a chicken can't be made
Without one.
Nor an alligator, a quail
A roach, a robin.
It's so compact
A shape that speaks of essence.
So strong for its weight, and perfectly suited
To the task.
Big or small, white, green, or speckled
It is the universal nurturer
Full of mystery.
The round inner halls
Full of potential... envision
A giant egg floating on the primeval ocean.
Where did it come from, that ocean and that egg?
No chicken has ever been big enough...
Maybe the Goddess laid it!

STORMY EVENING

That steamy hot evening, with
Clouds gathering in massive tribes,
We were leaving prosaic Topeka
(Not much beauty to be found)
And headed home
Into a wild wind
Veering from the southwest to southeast.

The temperature
Was dropping like the sun,
Brightly flirting and illuminating groups of trees
Or silver cars.
The lowest clouds were turning green and violet,
Alternately gorgeous
And ominously coiling.
The roadside trees
Were bowing and thrashing,
Yet still vibrant
In the glowing half light.

The first rolls of thunder
Were still miles away,
But the lightning was already putting on a show
That would put a rock concert to shame.
Before darkness fully fell
The rain came down
Darkening the rich greens of summer trees
And then, just hard, hard rain
Some small hail (in July!)
And a world reduced
To the size of windshield wipers' reach.

The lightning exalted me
The thunder called my name
As I was in a kind of trance.
It said "Your sacred name
Is Weather Woman."

RUNAWAY EARTH WORDS

Earth words can be heavy
Gray, like stone, like clay
Earth words can sprout
And bring forth surprises
As they flower in your mouth
Earth words are body words
Fat, thin, curved, straight
They can curl like vines
They can bear fruit
Or yield a poison
Earth words hold
All the elements
Fire, water, air, and love,
Earth words support us
And surround us
Earth words are life.

RIVER SONG

Rowing on the river, for the River itself, the
Boisterous song of the water, the River dolphins
Cavorting near me, the trees keeping their own
Deep green council on the banks
Rowing for the sky which graciously shelters me
And informs me of the weather, and rowing.

For the rising sun, the songs of other boatmen
And women, for the fish that will become my dinner
If the tables do not suddenly turn
Heading down that ratcheting, foaming river
With my heart pounding in my throat, praising
Life in every cell because there is nowhere to be
Except on this journey, this quest down the Amazon
With these companions, sweet and sour and tasty
As they are alive, wondering as I wonder
Hearing the falls ahead: inevitable and shining
And great as Death.

What am I rowing towards?
I can think only of the bliss of merging, the unbelievable,
Wonderful moment of surrendering
My individual consciousness into the Unknown
Seamless whole, into that Unknown,
Crashing over the falls, flying free as a raven
Straight into the sun. Does Death have a name?
What has that broken sack of bones peacefully gone for?
What has it gone for?
Down this river below the falls to do with me?

What am I now? I am the water and the bones
I am the raven and the dolphin. I am the voices
Of the River whispering and chuckling, roaring
In the ears of all the nearby children of Earth.
I am an artery that runs through the body of reality;
I bring fluid and growth, mud and floods. I am the delta
And the spirit of the Earth. Nothing left for me
Except to take my place in the whole.

UNTITLED

Agonized and weaving
Our elated weaving
Our exalted rugs of poetry
The warm shawl of words
That we wrap around our shivering unknowing
The brown earth belts we
Knit to hold us to the planet
Mother Earth belts that sprout green
Patterns as we grow through seasons
Then drop orange leaves
In the graveyard of our dreams
Where crows
Fly down to carrion
With their harsh sardonic laughs
And all our weaving seems
To be nothing but a quilt we
Leave our children's children

STORIES I HAVE HEARD OF BELTANE-BRIGID'S DAY

Spring has not yet spoken
Soft rains come, nothing much is greening
But the sheep have borne lambs.
Once again
The Wheel of the Year turns...
Enough milk for all!
And butter is made to glorify the rough bread
There is not much else to eat
Lucky trappers may get rabbits
The brined vegetables are long gone
The fruit trees may bud in a month or two
The grass will start to grow
Brigid was a real person, a Christian and a nun
She was a healer
She was an artist
She was a metalsmith and so much more.
She had a healing fountain that anyone could drink from
The pagans loved her well and she loved
Her people, all of them.
Perhaps she had lucid dreams
And followed her heart
She founded a nunnery
And outside the building an eternal flame
Was kept by her maidens... kept the sacred fire
Burning... even now! There were long forgotten miracles
She was a woman
She was a Goddess
She was Catholic as well
She was so much more!
Anyone could knock on her door...
Or so I have heard.

WHAT A MESS

Oh, say can you see
By the light of the sun
What a mess we have made
And the bad things we have done.
We have poisoned the earth
And the oceans are dying
In the service of greed
Our flag's long been flying
And the wars that we fight
They are often not right
They lie to us now
So we don't die of fright.

Oh, our nation is huge
With both beauty and power
We could truly help the world
If intelligence can flower.
When we let the farmers farm
And we cleaned up our act
Undo some of the harm
And save forests intact.

Oh, see can you say
We need to do it this way
When we swallow our fears
And are not ashamed to pray.

UNTITLED

I was leaning on a cottonwood
Just to watch the river run
Swallows darting here and there
Until the light of day was done
I fell into a reverie;
I was the water
The water was me
I flowed down the stream
A part of the whole
A part of the dream
Over rocks and over sand
Over boulders old and grand
Fish were swimming
Birds were skimming
Sometimes on the bottom
Sometimes on the top
Then the river threw me on the bank
And the "I" was just a single drop.
The sun came up
I was glistening on a flower
I longed for the river
And was hoping for a shower
The sun shone brightly
I was taken by the light
Became a part of a cloud
And the wind came, slight
At first, then stronger
We were blown south
Into a gray cloud bank
Heavy with water
And lighting zipping through
And there I was, a thunderstorm
And the rain was pounding down
First dripping
Then pouring
With lighting strikes
Then roaring and booming
Water cascading from the sky

Nothing underneath us
Could be dry
At first there was
A strange orange light
Something wrong for the middle of the night
Yet there was fire below.
I wondered was
There a God who would know?
Who burns down their forests and why?
And from my vantage in the sky
I dripped and dropped
And met the fire.
More clouds rolled in
Swollen with rain
Hurling it down
To that unfortunate plain
People and animals
Flowers and trees
Medicine plants and remedies
Endangered species
Mysterious and rare
Taking down the majestic forest
Leaving it smoky and bare.
I dived from the cloud
As the thunder clapped loud
My life as a drop
Was over
Perhaps I will come back
As a tear on the face
Of human disgrace

BEFRIENDING DEATH

There is nothing you can do about it
You might as well make friends!
After all, we have a life cycle.
Just like every living creature.
Our ego tells us
How special we are
How we, above all, deserve
To live a little longer
Take more resources
Demand busy other's attention
And of course, it is
Ego that causing the tension
Death, the dark shadow
Trailing along behind us,
Then suddenly
Your number is up!

What would it be like
To be friends with death?
I don't want it as a partner for chess
Or Scrabble, don't want it to dabble

In my relationships
I want it to stay away
From my family, my friends
But we all meet our ends
In these bodies...
In my case, worn out
Yet I have no doubt
I'll do some clinging
When I hear those bells ringing
I won't be extolling
The wonder of living
As I hear my breath heaving
My small family grieving
I feel like he's thieving
That cold morbid death
Will be the death of me yet.

ALL SPECIES PARTY

Please! Peace... Let's invite
The vanishing creatures
And use the red foil tablecloths
Food and drink for all species
As well as mantras, words of power
And protection
Some psychoactive plants
Let's throw a party!

All will be spoken and translated
In all the different voices
"Hi, I am a transgender dog!
Ho— I'm a phylogenetic frog,
An anthropologist"
"And I am Count Love Bite
Vampire bat... don't worry— I ate
Before I came. Plenty of humans
Are joining the fun
There will be a story corner
And flaming peace at the campfire.

Swami Sivananda Banda
Will conduct kundalini session
For any and all species
And if you come up with a brilliant plan
To save the last spotted owl
Or the most threatened Mexican wolf
You could win ten thousand dollars!
Even if you don't, your heart will be happy
The best party ever!

UNTITLED

My body on hers
Weeping, digging in my hands
Always, she comforts.

Garden, I scratch you
Tuck the seeds in with a song
Trusting the good soil.

How do you do it?
Producing food and flowers
Once again this year.

BOA AND JAGUAR

Boa
Huge snake I fear you
Huge snake I revere you
Devour me if you will
Then live, curled or uncurled
At the base of my spine
And speak to me of elemental power.

Boa says nothing, sends vision
Sounds and colors swirling
Bizarre reptilian tang of metal and carnivore shit
Suddenly, I see through her jeweled eyes
The jungle, the river, the skies.

Jaguar
Shadow flowing through trees
Muscles powerful and loose
Running through a landscape
Of blood and flowers
Primal bliss, part of the spirit
No pain, no guilt, no fear.

Jaguar says:
Be negative space
See how everything shines
Around you.

UNTITLED

The crocuses are saying:
Here we come, we push
Our green stems up proudly
As our buds form
Under the caress of sun
We were not afraid of the cold
Our root toes are happy in the damp cold mud
We feel our colors growing
We will not wait for the tulips
Or the henbit
We are purple, yellow, full of rebirth
Here we come

I AM FOR LOVE

I am from love
I am wrapped in love
I am warped in love
I love my love
My love is lived
My love is lively
Love makes it better
Love is the one
Who writes a letter
Love is when
I sit by the water
Love the brown/green river
And the hedge trees
The sweet grass, butterflies
Cloud-painted ever-changing skies
The city in the distance
That has taken me in
I love friends and families
The plants and the animals
I am blessed (and sometimes cursed)
To live and die
On this sacred battered earth

IN NOVEMBER

In November
Frigid fields with lonely weeds
Little birds everywhere
Gleaning last traces of harvest
Wetland pools are silvery gray
Ruffling in the North wind.
Pelicans, geese, fly down to fish
As if they no longer know
Just when and where to migrate.
I can't wait for winter holidays
To come and go... nowadays they carry
Too much weight
The joys and sorrows of past years
The fears of what may be coming
Christmas carols on the radio
Still bring this old pagan to tears
I get back under the comforter
Joints aching fiercely— just before sleeping
My closed eyes see a flash of vivid green
Reminds me that spring too will return
The Goddess will return.

HARVEST

The garden spiders sit and spin
Honey's in the comb, corn is gathered in
Honeydew juice runs down my chin...

Two blocks from my house, at the edge of a suburban cornfield
A gentle woman deer drew last breath, sank gracefully down
To her mother earth... as my nostrils fill with death stench
Her bones are excavated by a teeming team of maggots, one hoof
Pointed skyward like a message.

Later, full moon rises on a warm primal August night, hazy skies
And half-seen meteor showers, or curling into sleep
The last image entering open eyes a sky full of lightning, then
Waking up to fog light, sun burns obliquely
People loom up like shadow puppets, and the valleys swallow traffic.

Early morning spider spins
Her sticky threads are pulling us in
We're all in the web— we are her kin— weaving the weaving of life
And breath, dancing the pattern of seasons and death.
Fog burns off, leaves Sunflower day
Demeter is still at play, though Persephone must soon
Go underground, the goddess left grieving
Through long winter round.

Harvest is bountiful, there are stores for what's ahead
Sacred wine is in the bottle, grain is in the shed
The first brown leaves surrender... the gentle deer is dead.

I PLEDGE ALLEGIANCE

I pledge allegiance
To the roots
At home in the Mother, taking nourishment
And giving it
To the plants above, which proudly stand
Tree, vegetable, fruit, or herb
Silently enjoying life
Making breathable air,
Feeding every body
Dancing with the wind
At one with the cycle
Of life and death.

I pledge my love
To the Earth Mother
From her mighty cliff bones
To the wisdom of her
Changing moods, the seasons.

I walk with her in snow and rain
Her winds caress me
Or challenge me, they
Whisper wisdom
I lie on her in spring
Giving her my tears
As she gives me violets.

COTTONWOOD

Cottonwood likes to stand by the river
Sinks tree-root toes into running water
Grows fast, tall and sturdy, with leaves all a-quiver
Holds up her branches, the sun's fine daughter

Cottonwood makes sticky buds in the spring
Magical buds for making a potion
Carries them high so you can't reach a thing
Plays with the wind and murmurs in motion

Cottonwood dreams by the river in the heat
Her seeds float like gossamer stars
Her leaves, great green hearts, their rustling so sweet
You start to dream too, of a life with no wars

To love cottonwood, go lie on the shore
South wind will whisper— you'll ask to know more

UNTITLED

It always wheels to this
The seasons of reaping and dying
The long cold, huddled-in-the-heart cave
Dreaming deep green dreams.
When darkness fell, the sparrows rustled
In the bamboo, while two young sharp-shinned
Hawks always found their dinner.

I look back at my good red road, seeing
The weary miles traversed.
The sun is low in the west
Warming the chambers of my crone-seeing heart
Opening me to what's ahead
The sunset and then the starry darkness.

HAND ME DOWNS

HAND ME DOWNS

From my father
I got the Germanic skull,
The tendency to redden.
I got his storytelling gene
And the pain he hid
Until it ate him alive at 51.
I got the luxury of seeing the stars
And the actual Milky Way
Deep in the country in 1950
From the haven of his lap
As he taught me constellations.
My brother got the cars, the tools
But Dad forced him to give up the violin
Which ended up decades later
In my daughter's hands.
I saw him in myself, finding my male side
But not liking it much.

From my Grandmothers I was handed down
Memories, all mostly good, and a few recipes.
My mother handed me her religion, incessantly.
She backed up her spirituality
With impressive charity and kindness.
I choked on her visions
Of Heaven and Hell
And voyeuristic Father God
But years later, I have her ability to love
Most people I meet, and make them comfortable.
I have her drive to connect constantly
With the Divine.

From my sister
I got so much
I cannot even list it.
She fostered me
And fed my brain
My eyes, ears, and hands; my
Imagination.

From my brother I got mean teasing,
But he would never let anyone else tease me.
He played classical music in his room
And it drifted into mine.
I have never stopped loving the magic created by composers.
I stole five silver dollars from his room
To go to the fair.... he must have known it was me
But I did not confess and apologize... it took me forty years!

MY LIFE AS KALEIDOSCOPE

Ceaselessly opening, unfolding
Patterns that fly out to edges
Or collapse upon themselves.
No opening into color or clear light
Stays, no diving into deep dark center
Becomes a still point
I open to anchor and flux.

When my daughters came through me
I screamed on cusp of orgasmic pain
Then their ravenous baby mouths
Tirelessly seeking my nipples.
Shattering, I stretched, opened my heart
And never could stop. While kaleidoscope
Dissolves into something greater
Not just patterns
But an infinite falling
Into the country of love.

FOR MY SISTER

What brought me to this river?
What pulled me to this sunrise?
Only the voices of the winged ones answer
As red sun pulls light from darkness
Landscape colors chase each other
Across the cliffs in harmonies of buff, pink,
Crimson. I came here because you died.
Perhaps I though river would murmur an answer
To this thorny, intractable pain,
Would guide me as words could not
To the central core of why.

Now full day illuminates ashes of last
Night's fire, a small breeze dances comfort
To my hot, sad face. I let the voices of the river
Draw me closer, until finally I plunge into the water
Begging for a cleansing from this mortal grief.

The water slaps me with its stinging cold
And the current is stronger than I thought
Soon, I am swimming for my life, grabbing
Slippery rocks, grasping, gasping, praying.

Back at the bank, dripping and shivering
My body sings with every cell
I am alive!
In mind's eye I see your face
Your wise laughing eyes, I hear you whisper
From that formless place
"Use my death to love your life!"

UNTITLED

Feeling groggy—
Let's talk about
Beautiful yesterdays
Since the cultural, moral void
Is swelling, essential references
We shared in common are now missing,
Replaced with air showers
Of empty endless media words.
I want to go back
To grandma's amazing cast iron kitchen.
She made food for up to twelve
And finally, down to two
Every day, three times a day—
Chicken and dumplings, cornbread and molasses
Wild greens and rice, her famous apple cake
And the best fresh bread with the best name—
Light bread! After she died, I dreamed her
Gleaming white-haired angel
Holding out another loaf of light.

GENTLE CYCLE

Born into this strangely violent reality
I remember from toddlerhood
My mother weeping for the boys in Korea
My parents worried murmuring
About the Mideast.

At school, we practiced hiding
From tornadoes and then the bomb
We were all pretty sure by third grade
That arms over heads wouldn't save us.
At recess we chased the stinky boy
Threw sand in his eyes
Because his butt smelled bad
On the way home, we battled with sticks.

But there were gentle cycles
Waves of living peacefully
Eating grandma's chocolate pudding,
Making small play homes in the bushes
Bouquets for my sister
Riding my bike all the way uptown.

Married, with children
Most days brought conflict
I wasn't enough
He was too much or we switched roles
Money was scarce
And work was brutal
He killed rabbits and I had to cook them
We took our children into our landlord's field
To eat corn straight from the plant.
Nearly everyday someone was screaming.

But then there were gentle cycles
When lovemaking got us through
When we remembered what to do
When the baby disarmed us
When our daughters were precious
And life seemed more spacious.

THE WELL

The village wells where all the women
Used to gather, talk and laugh
Gossip and quarrel
All the while drawing up the water
For their families.
Today we still need that community well
Because things are welling up in us, because
Things are welling up, because
Women and water are two forces of nature.
Powerful, nourishing, yet able to go with the flow
We still need to meet at the well, draw up
Water that plumps out our skin, refreshes
Our spirits, releases
Our own waters of emotion.
We need to laugh and cry
With our sisters, help each other carry
The burdens, yes, we need to drink deep of
That holy water.

FOR JOANNE

In the days of the mid nineteen-forties,
my father served
as a metalsmith on a huge war boat
and he nearly died of an appendectomy gone
riot, and my mother lived in a humble
cabin near a beautiful mountain in Oregon.
Joanne was the eldest and my brother, Victor,
also very young— his comment to the existence
of a little sister: "I want a puppy!"

Joanne, age nine, was ecstatic for a baby sister
and quickly started responding to my needs.
She never stopped teaching me in life, happily
taught me song after song, and we sang
Christian hymns to folk songs
and my slowly healing father offered songs as well.
Joanne turned out to be the smartest person in our
family; left for college at sixteen and
on to grad school where she earned
a double degree in Chicago for both criminology and
Christian counseling.
This Christian thing was something
I did not share with her, and she never pushed.

She and her husband produced two children, a girl and
a boy.
I know the girl much better of the two, and I am so glad to know her!
Back to the story— after a fascinating life into
middle age, cancer snuck up on her.
She was SO ALIVE!
She was the family member I could talk to about
ANYTHING! And I needed her.

I loved her equanimity, her understanding.
I traveled to her from Kansas in her last days.
I sang all the songs she had taught me, hymns and all.
I held her hands and planned to be there until she let go,
but soon her husband asked me to leave so I had to go.
All I can say is she is a part of me, and so is her daughter.

VISION

This woman's big— she dances
With confidence and joy. She's not
Young; her neck says she has bent before
And not just once. You wouldn't
Call her pretty, she is beautiful as a holy person
Her head expanding into light.
Big hands gesturing and freeing
She is singing the mantra
She is dancing the mantra
She is chanting in the green light
The mantra of "I am."

Sister, you are gray, yet too radiant
To be a ghost— you are made
Of blue clay and starlight
Which life do you speak from?
My own beautiful sister is long dead
Fiercely missed— in life she loved, she wrote
She danced as you do
She sang the mantra "I am!"

MOTHER

Waking at dawn to the radio, my bed still wet
at six years old, my mother weeping.
At first, I thought she wept for another sheet to wash but
it was for the world— many had died in a tornado
the night before.

Early memories: disappearing as regular as the sun
in her Dodge Dart, working at the phone company.
I watched her go, then sat in her closet
where shoes piled like leaves, hats and clothes smelled
of her perfume.

Every evening she read the Bible, then we prayed.
My only comic book was the life of Jesus.
The Bible wasn't the only book. There was the Reader's Digest
and always Mother's new romance book— clean and sweet, with
no sex but
I read them all.

She liked to help; my mother delivered the baby
next door, took food to Mrs. Bagwell, whose mattress
actually WAS stuffed with money when she died.

Mom brought home orphans from the church, treated
them like daughters, much to my disgust.
She was gracious, conventional, kind,
considered the neighborhood Wise Woman.
Her family saw how fierce she could become
if backed into a corner, or if a child's welfare was at stake.

We called her the Ma-Bear and love her spirit to this day.

ON BEING A YOUNG GIRL IN KANSAS SPRINGTIME

To My Daughters—

Never forget you're a prairie girl
Rooted here by your grandmothers
And great-grandmothers,
Who also stood
Fresh cheeked and fifteen
In Kansas springtime sun
Who hid in cornfields
Giggling, kissed and breathless
Who peered uncertain
From dark sod houses of their ignorance,
Who cried as you
Cry, and stubbornly learned
To take their power.

Never forget your grandmothers
One, baptized in Holy Spirit
Carried the stream of her immersion
Always with her, walked with the Lord,
Touched lives...
The other followed the rhythms
Of her small sturdy body
To a jazzy life of music
In a twinkling coastal city
Then returned to bear children
All three cut from her womb.

Your grandmothers could not have
Dreamed your life –
Who could've seen
(From grimy Dust Bowl days
And the brutal depths of the
Depression) the end of the 20th century?
They could not comprehend
Your freedom, your outrageous
Naughtiness,
Your scorn!

One, in desperation
Might have cut a willow switch
Taken it to tender backs of knees
All the while praying to her Jesus
To touch your proud,
Your stubborn heart.
The other would've cried
Shocked and helpless in a
World of acid trips, mosh pits
And casual bisexuality.

UNTITLED

Dear Universe—
I learned to love you
On my grandpa's farm
So far away from urban light
Dark magnificent sight
Sky, stars, and milky way
Five years old on my father's lap
Learning the names and constellations
And stories
Seeing the moon
In all of its glowing glory
And all of the phases—
What wonderful grace it is
Riding in a car
Moon pursuing you everywhere,
Then forgetting from afar.

Dear Earth—
I cannot express your worth
Books could be filled
With your beauty
I have been here with you since my birth
A very young girl
So happy to whirl
And dance with south wind
I did not want to go in
For dinner.
I was a girl that climbed your trees
Completely at ease
'Til mom said "You cannot show your panties!"
So I threw my dress
And asked for jeans
They didn't understand
How much it means
To me, the holy ground
All around, just asking to be dug
My friends and I
At the moonlit park nearby
Chasing those magic sparks.

AFTER THE FUNERAL

I dreamed you were among the dead
Shimmering with spirit light
In and out of my sight
Not in your body in a way I could recognize
Nor completely parted from it.

Your beard's shadow still clung to your chin
A suggestion of glasses, a nose aquiline
And you were still anxious
Wandering the bardos in the dark red light
"Where did everybody go?
I need to be with my family."
The bills, the insurance, the doctor appointments.
The pain still hovered around you
The inexorable years of illness
At last, you weren't worried about breathing anymore.

I dreamed you were among the dead
I called to you with desolate longing
I know you could feel me
Thought a misty curtain was between us
I knew I was holding you
When I should, for mercy's sake,
Let you go.

HOW TO SAVOR
A DAY

SO MANY COLORS STILL UNSUNG

A girl went out to see the sky
And went inside to paint it.
The paper would not hold the truth
But she thought she could fake it.
Only she knew that infinity is blue
And also black as void, shiny as crow's feathers
Sparkling like Los Angeles at night.
Try as she might, her colors ran and bled
And refused to tell the story. She moved on
To live her life in the garbage and the glory.

A woman went out to see the earth, and brought
Her brushes with her. She sought to flow
The season's hues on paper in the weather.
When her paintings dried she wept,
A tiny little flood... the grays and browns were
Dead as lead, her tears were rust and blood.

This woman thought to paint her friends
Their beauty and their fear... with line
And shape and texture, she hoped to make it clear
Just what she saw and hoped to share.
Her paintings were arresting, but the subtleties
Were gone. Her friends appeared as harlequins
Or with the soul light gone.

This woman now is aging fast; her hands
Are getting stiff. She sees her fate approaching
And dreams of doom and death
There's little chance of capturing
The colors of the world.
Her eyesight slowly spiraling into the vibrant dark.
Her spirit also floats, and waits, and speculates: how many colors
Left unsung?

IT MAY NOT BE SEX

It may not be sex, but when hummingbirds
Plunder the deep red throats of blossoms,
Their little bodies like winged jewels, barely
Contained by the material plane, when
Butterflies unfurl their spiral tongues to sip
Sweet juices and bumble bees labor
In love with swollen pink nubs of clover
It's hard not to notice: Universe makes love
To itself constantly.

It may not be sex, but the milky bliss
Of babies nuzzling at the breast
Will elude them for that original flavor, neither
Chocolate nor vanilla. Meantime their mothers
Embarrassed by their own deep pleasure
Wonder why no one ever mentions
How profoundly good it feels.

In India, ancient sages speak of Amrita, a
Kind of nectar drink in states of deep
Meditation; Amrita secreted by pineal gland
At the base of the brain, drops into throat, is harvested
By tongue turned back on itself to soft palate!
To taste is to know: we ourselves are none other
When scales drop from our eyes, we are leaves
Shuddering from the touch of their wild wind lover.
We are snakes adoring earth with their scaled bellies.
We are eternal: water, honey, breast milk, semen, stars.

You may not call it sex but Universe
Just never stops for a single nanosecond.
Universe makes love to itself constantly!

THE BEST FOOD IN THE WORLD

Is eaten with your lover,
On a river bank is good
Or a park very huge
Call it a picnic.
Bring ripe berries and soft cheese
Artisan bread, chocolate
You need good olives, maybe hard
Boiled eggs, a twist of salt, a bottle
Of wine, the best you can afford.
And just one blanket, meant for kissing, passing blackberries
From mouth to mouth, you may pick
Some wild weeds, the tender wild
Violet blossoms, your breasts will become
Fluffy clouds to support your beloved
His body calls to yours, the taste of wine
Is on your breast, and afterward,
An Altoid or two.

PENTIMENTO

I painted that painting
Now I am painting it again.
Those blues were too dark, too raw
The water pulled in darkness
And did not reflect.
The sky dense and awkward
With clotted cream clouds.
A white bird flies up the cliff
But looks like a paper cutout
The mesas are too bright
In browns, oranges, and reds.
Making the greens clash and not shelter
I painted that painting
In fifteen-minute intervals
Grabbed between kitchen duties
And too exhausted to create.
No easel available, so I prop it
On a plastic chest which holds crackers
So that nearly every day
Some hungry one
Moves the painting to the floor
Now it has sulked by the closet
For quite a while
Just asking for a redo, some quality time
With the artist.
Now I see clearly— it's not just the blues that are wrong
It's ALL the colors, excepting the sienna
And umbers of the mesas.
I put a thin white wash down
So everything is seen through a curtain.
In the misty light of the drying wash
The white bird is taking flight.

SCENTS AND NON-SENSE

I believe in sniffing the sweet
Heads of new babies
The fragrance of a healthy horse
Flowering trees in springtime
Are like a river of scent.
And the glorious smells of food
Could fill a life, mythic soup steam
Bread baking, garlic, lemons, sesame and thyme
Oranges and sausages, campfire coffee on
A frosty morning, bacon and trout in a pan
I loved the scent of my husband, healthy male sweat,
Fragrant oils, and he liked the sexy ones,
Old Spice and cigarettes evoke my father
As words cannot. Leaving smell, I find that taste
Is intimately connected; I am ravenous for a taste
Of Key Lime pie, raspberries, fresh asparagus
And morels... pasta bathed in fruity green olive oil
Fresh basil, freshly grated Parmesan, and that
Ubiquitous garlic presence, some salt.
Chocolates from Godiva, truffles melting on the palate
Filled with exotic surprises... hot roasted cashews!
When it comes to skin, what could be better than your
Lover's loved skin against yours? The delicate inside of
One's wrist grazing the softest skin, lips teasing lips!
Ah, the memories of those wonderful arms around us
Only water comes close, hot tub, cold stream
Warm shower, herbal steam. Or sitting in an unbelievably
Hot sauna with others in my tribe, a happy monkey!

BORDERLINE

I've always loved the seamless way
Reality blends into itself, the blurred
Edges on every horizon.
My suburb gives way to tiny houses returning
To earth, ditches and fertile fields
Places for the dreaming mind to wander.

I like the sometimes way a casual kiss
Crosses the line into blood heat and roses
Or driving, one sees a stranger
In an old VW bus, and easily start falling
Into a different story than the one
You have always told yourself.

I like the places all of us go that are neither
Winter nor Spring, full sleeping
Or full wakening, the place between two
People where it is never yes or no
But always a maybe,
Trembling with possibility.

EARLY DAYS, LATE DAYS

It was nearly late May sundown
The day had scorched the lake water
Still warm in the shallows
We were celebrating high school graduation
My friends around me, I ran into the water first
Aroused by their collective beauty, unaware
Of any I might have possessed
I dug my bare feet into cool sand
The water just covered me up to my bra
Much cooler than I thought— my mind
Emptied— their talk and laughter far away
I stood directly in the ground of being
While a school of tiny fish (none had graduated)
Surrounded me with gentle bumps and nibbles
All of them tasting me softly with their wee
Piscean mouths! Incapable of speech
I gave no explanation
Just hoped against hope that no one
Had noticed my moans
I already had a reputation for weirdness—
Just hoped no one noticed that sun, fish, water, and a world of such
    bliss
Had given me an orgasm!

ZEN POOPING

No need to read or use the phone
When thoughts arise just let them go
Sit well at ease on porcelain throne
There's nothing special you must know.

Don't push and strain or grunt and groan
And don't get purple in the face
Just concentrate on the bowel koan
Let gentle gravity set the pace.

You seekers of the Buddha's bliss
This humble act, do not disdain
Just meditate on emptiness
Enlightenment can't be contained.

Remember not to get too haughty
Even Bodhisattvas use the potty!

PARCHED

My parched being yearns— as hummingbird to blossom— to sip
Your sweet lips, then fearlessly dive deep
Into waters I can't fathom.
Where emotions are colored fish and shocking creatures lurk
Waiting to electrify.

My parched being, yearning through endless desert
Grows thorns to survive, yet dreams a rosy baby dream
In which my mouth finally reaches, greedily, your breast
And you feed me, like a mother.

My trembling body, living on tiniest mercy drops
Follows the casual trail of crumbs you leave: your embraces,
Soft words, our little stolen kisses...
Ah, it inflames but does not sustain
And when I come upon your heartdoor
I find a wall of shame.

COLORS

Speaking from the adult
And from the wounded child
Weaving that speaking together
Weaving a pattern from the eternal womb of poetry.

Red raw threads of pain against the concrete
Grays of daily life
Sun gold flashes of inspiration
Silver shards of what we felt in full moonlight
Black and indigo passages
For all the times we stumble, clueless in the dark.

Pink and violet ripples
Pulsating from the heart of us
Beating like clockwork
Beating rhythms from the center of everything
Informing the cadences of our agonized weaving
The warm shawl of words
That we wrap around our shivering unknowing.

The brown earth belts that sprout green patterns
As we grow through the seasons
Then drop orange leaves in the graveyards of our dreams
Where crows fly down to carrion
With their harsh sardonic laughter
And all our weaving seems
To be nothing but a quilt we leave
To our children's children.

HERBAL MAGIC

The best herbal magic
makes you feel that God may be love,
at least for a couple of hours.
The ganja, the good green medicine,
smooths out the wrinkles in your play,
breaks down some walls, opens
the eye of your eyes, the ear of your ears.

Music dances you and you whirl
in cosmic space.
The stars twinkle messages
that will be lost tomorrow.
Your body drops tension like a shower of coins
and drapes itself out in sensual grandeur.
Traffic turns into a background hum
and you hear the grasshoppers and cicadas singing.

You are attracted to simple things— fire and water,
grass and moonlight. You forget you can't sing
and you sing, sing and laugh and the last thing
in the world you take seriously is yourself.
You can do anything, cook without a recipe, paint,
cry, lick your friends and LAUGH as if the world
were a safe and friendly place;
pain sulks in a back alley of consciousness
and awaits its comeback.
Ganja, the good green herb— one of my oldest friends!

MEAT

All those incarnations squatting by the fire,
Gnawing the fat, bone, juice running
Down face, hunter/hunted, smart animal plotting
Shaman dancing, dancing in bearskin,
Antelope leather, hungry people make
Magic pictures of fat buffalo on cave walls,
Mouth watering, being woman, humble, pregnant, chewing on desperate
    roots, bitter berries, waiting for arrogant males to throw her a bone.

Scrabbling in stream, hands numb in cold, looking for water food,
Running through trees, checking little traps and snares
But oh, when hunters return, everyone's face is smeared with fat
Toothless old women of thirty, DNA memory, tooth memory, mouth
    longings, tongue needs.
Looking in my mirror, an ancient wrinkled face peers back at me
With dark brown eyes, she is bone woman.
This woman is never satisfied
This female ancestor stakes her claim,
Says: "Gnaw. Chew. Dribble. Lick. Devour."

To this woman meat is intimate as the song of blood
This one is devouring her own tissue, casually chews her tongue
This one is me, incarnations, overlays of civilized times
Not rhino bones, no bear paw soup, no blubber, not even squirrel,
    snake or mouse.
Internal organs disgust me. I'll not eat the brain or kidney of another
    creature.
No thanks to tripe and heart.
My higher self is waking.
I'd rather starve than eat a whale.
My higher self is stirring.

Inner voice says: Don't eat your fellow creatures!
Be healthy, happy, wise on tofu, vegetables.
Fruits give their life for you with love and acceptance.
Animals too give gifts.
When the Moon is full, my rational brain says:
Iron. Calcium.
My inner guide whispers, sweetly of beans and rice and the third world
Ah but when my heart aches, that ancient unrepentant child in me says:

MEAT. MEAT. MEAT.

YOU, READER

Be glad there are still books
Poems like beacons to light
Your moment, and carry you, changed
Into the next.
Be glad for your eyes, the simple human
Pleasure of reading, the sharing
Of a stranger's thoughts
And how they echo or beckon, or repel
Be glad there is a world, where you
May sit or lie at leisure, think of how
You inhabit form, how energy coalesces
And shapes into lips and hands, trees
And rivers, hearts and minds.
Feel the rivers running through you
And the ones you would dive into
Be so thankful for the coyote watching you
Invisible
The snake swimming
Through remembered creeks of childhood.
The running of deer. Someday the earth
We know will most definitely be gone
And you, reader,
Will also be gone.

THE ART CRITIC

This art I saw is dark, brilliant
Profoundly nonverbal.
The piece I like the best,
The darkest and most abstract
Reminds me very much
Of my inner world, the place I go
When I shut my eyes, focus on breath
And relax into the void...
At first, so dim, one strains to see content
Then, as I gaze into the space between
My eyebrows, as if I am looking
Into my own brain, just gazing
The focus changes, and there is actually
So much light, subtle, ever changing
Quiet and lovely, so much activity
Seeing the atomic dance of energy
Quite directly, and as I behold it
The bottom drops out, and I am sitting
In the void, which is mine, both personal
And impersonal... I am sitting in the dance
Of energy, of which I am a part,
Completely supported by only my breath,
And by the fabric of the universe... I gaze
I breathe, and this is as much as I know
Of infinity.

MIDLIFE CRISIS NUMBER THREE

In a season of storms and rainbows
Love filled my mouth like ripe raspberries
Plucked with stinging fingers
From your overflowing vines,
Juices running down my face.

In a summer of hot urgency
Tomatoes bursting on the vine
Desire filled my body like a throbbing
Bassline, making me dance
Ecstatic and pain filled, bewildered as a bear
Caught and tamed to prance its supper.
Bare breasted in a strange kitchen
I washed dishes in the double heat
Of August and passion.

Your quicksilver beauties filled my eyes
Inscribed my skin with tattoos
Where your casual fingers brushed...
I wanted to break free, new feelings filled me
Like floodwater, too much to contain
Dripping from my eyes as tears
Flowing from my mouth as laughter
Filling that aching void
Between my legs.

Mercurial summer, heat and rain, gardens rampant
With the food and flowers. My life stopped being ordinary.
In the space where our eyes met
A nameless emotions sparked energy in all directions.
In the infinite space of the heart chakra
Seagulls cried and hurled themselves at desolate rocks.

MOSAICS

Colored bits of information
Fixed in place with skill and art
'Til shapes and colors come together
The whole is greater than the parts.
We find strange scenes
Millennia later
Still sparkling with stories to relate.
The Roman gods in sartorial splendor
Or ocean creatures
Octopus and the skate.

I think my life is a mosaic
Creating patterns I can't see
All these bits of information
Together form reality.

While my big picture
Is still in the making
I will think that I'm swimming
Or possibly baking, I might be
Breaking my neck or having great sex
The matriarch of a clan
Or pandering to a man
Playing with my descendants
Trying for transcendence

Each tile of reality
Glows with meaning
Then the light moves on
Put a picture in a photo album
Remember me when I am gone.

WHAT WE LEARN FROM FACES

First, the eyes, we meet with our own
Then glance back to the brows for anger
Consternation or surprise
Then back to the eyes: obsidian, giving nothing
Away, dark brown twinklers flirt and change,
An enigma! The blues are limpid
Somehow more naked... some do say you should
Never trust a blue-eyed man! But for me
There are beauties that I love to scan
The grays are calm and steady, but storms
Can swiftly build. Green and Hazel can bewitch
Or sizzle with excitement...
From the nose we learn less
Unless Pinocchio's legend is true
We may see the long, pointed ones
As poking in our beeswax, and we can view
The snubs, fair or not, as a tendency to pig out...
Really, though unless it's red and wet with snot
The nose enlightens not.
Mouths are mobile, full of changes
Smiles as bright as Christmas night
Can turn so quickly to anger or fright!
Our mouths know when another wants to kiss
It can be a problem just to deal with this!
Now we come to chins and ears
With them there is little to fear
Fat chins jiggle, big ears wiggle, lobes
Hold weight and dangle
But from any angle
They are no more than flesh!

TERMINAL NOSTALGIA

Is this the nostalgia you feel
As you enter the terminal one last time
With your hopefully two-way ticket,
"Straight to death" and back?
That would be a nostalgia greater than any other
Remembering even the insignificant days, the difficult
Nights, the wins and losses (with loss winning)
Pleasure laced with pain
You want the natural world! The body!
However flawed and sticky
You will remember the bird-sung dawns
Of kindergarten, snakes swimming in streams
Moonlight kisses
Primal embraces, howling
Music, places
People who still love you
(How will they do without you?)
Ready or not, here comes the train!

FERMENT

Fine pickles
Excellent wines and spirits
Roiling around inside me
Myself giving space to this bubbly process
Earthy and joyful, dance of good bacteria
Not always on the material plane
Things transform themselves.

Forgive me
Everyone, I am unable to form whole sentences
Really
Magical
Energy is brewing in my psyche
Never know what kind of product
To expect from this batch
It's just too exciting
Night will fall
Grandly, in Technicolor before I taste it.

I
Never
Expected how good it would be.

Pretty colors
Icebox pickles
Cabbage into kimchi
Kitchen magic
Let's
Eat
Some!

INFINITE SLEEP HORIZON

Inside my head the sleepy stars
Dance and twinkle
And light is a surreal orange glow
On a vast horizon of darkness
The people too are dark
Their tiny candles like fireflies
I hear their shining voices
Five billion miles away
As they trek ever onward
Voices on the edge of the known universe
The children sing a shrill soprano pure note
The women full of passion and mourning
The men's deep rumbling
Elemental, raw as thunder
Their song is eternal
My brain is one with the infinite sun
Their song is an electronic piping
In my right ear, so subtle
I must enter the silence to hear it
In singing silence, I enter the world of dreams

THE WORK OF DREAMS

The work of dreams
Is wondrously strange
Your sleeping mind has such a range
Of stuff and nonsense, it seems.
Your daily life is minced to bits
The pieces mixes with psychic trash
Fears and myths and archetypes clash
And interact in starts and fits.
Why do we do it? Why is it so thrilling?
(We're not necessarily willing.)
We can't just eschew it.
We don't just dream, the dreams dream us
They set our brains afloat
And nightmares come from bloat—
We don't just scream, the dreams scream at us.
The work of dreams
Is Jungian and fierce
Our fantasies are pierced
It is not what it seems.

DON'T TELL ANYONE!

My hair is magical
(Long brown and silver shaggy mane)
It knits itself together in the Southwest wind; I am
Dreaded like an elf-child
Ponytail behind me in a stubborn tangled bush.
I wash it in desert herbs (gently, not much suds)
No dryer for this fine thin hair.
Next morning the magic begins to build: even
With conditioner the knots are a tangible
Record of my pain. Beginning with the scalp
I rake my fingers through each handful, again
And yet again, running them out to the limits,
Clearing obstacles, cleansing anxiety
It takes thirty minutes, the under layer still damp
And when my fingers, stiff but still serviceable, meet
No obstacles, my head is glowing like a Celtic
Goddess surrounded by an aura of dancing particles
Fire in the head! I pick up the brush
And tease out every trouble, breathe in conscious
Air, hear inner crickets singing
I feel the fine feathery currents of energy
With the sensitive tips of my hair.
Next, I anoint my scalp with a salve
That smells of pears, waft it through
With my brush of animal hair.
I am old, my beauty is gone, but I put
My black teddy on
And my hair wafts messages of love on the ground
In a forgotten orchard with bees... it draws my beloved
Near. My hair is magical
It has its own powers.

EARTH MOTHER SOUP

Have you heard about my wonderful homemade soup?
It's better than grandma's, better than your mom's
Oh, theirs could tame the common virus as well
As my Japanese garlic broth
But my soup is magical.
If I need company, I start to sauté
Onions and celery in my special pot
And within the hour, wandering husbands
Appear, friends drop by
Adult children return home with loads of laundry,
Stay to spoon down nostalgic bites of childhood.

Chicken, vegetable, or cream of Tuesday
You can smell it all over town, and
My soup expands on command.
Potato bisque for four can feed twelve if necessary.
Vegetable stew reinvents itself
With cream and extra peas
To sustain the midnight travelers
Just in from Boulder.
Are your feet cold?
My cayenne tomato rice will heat you in a hurry.

Or if you're feeling needy
You can be greedy, glom a gob of noodles
Fragrant with parsley, tarragon, and thyme.
I am a Queen of matzo ball soup
Every Passover two big pots:
One traditional and full of schmaltz
One vegetarian, floating with carrots
In a lemon-herb broth.
People schlep down those dumplings
Like there's no tomorrow—
And I'm not even Jewish!

I came from the proud tradition
Of stone-soup makers.
Give me a rock, a pot, and some
Stories, the random leaf or root or fish—

I'll give the village
A kettleful of sustenance
A belly full of liquid joy.

You may be asking yourself
Why is HER soup so good?
I will share my secrets.
It's not too difficult,
But it does take time.
It helps if you have eaten Grandma's Depression recipe
Crumbling saltines into steaming childhood bowls
Of plain old potato or onion,
Taking in history like a kind of edible knowledge.

Grown at last, you need some poverty of your own.
Get on a first-name basis with powdered
Eggs and government Spam.
Search your yard while massively pregnant for edible greens.
Experiment extensively with soybeans and brown rice
Garnished with produce from the Safeway dumpster.
Realize you must grow a garden
And struggle for years
When it's ten times as hard as you thought.

Have children, and
Rise to the occasion of filling
Their bellies
Again and again and again.
Become so one-pointed
That their friends show up, and feed them too.

Learn to use everything you have
And when it's still a little short
You'll have no choice except magic
To make it stretch and fill.
Make soup from gourmet cookbooks
Then give away the books.
Search your heart for the recipe
That will tempt your dying mother,
Season liberally with tears.

Somewhere in all this making
You'll learn to be patient and grateful
Find yourself thanking the carrots
Sending the chicken to the light.
You can now take
Strange dried roots from the Chinese grocery
Make a broth from seaweed and soy sauce
Cream of pumpkin or turnip
Any old thing that comes into your hands
And turn it into glorious food.

Now you have heard about my Earth Mother soup—
Come on over for a bite.

BITTERSWEET

Life can be as sweet as the head of a newborn baby
Or a rose blooming out of season
An unexpected compliment
Holding hands with ones we love... puppies
Licking our faces... life can hold untold surprises
Which make us cry or smile
But always, we walk another mile
And turn another corner
And then clouds block the sun
You are angry with someone
Your plans did not go right
You are left behind and out of sight
The poetics of trauma kick down the door
You feel you can't be happy any more
You look down at your feet
And the world is bittersweet
You are yearning for the past
But the future never lasts... the baby is twenty-four
Already walked right out the door
Or your beloved one changes his tune.
As you cry beneath the moon
You know that there is beauty
And you're feeling mighty moody
Like you never got the goodies
Then you did, and they tasted bad, bittersweet.

HOW TO SAVOR A DAY

Wake up naturally
When the sun taps your closed lids
Stretch before you leave the bed
If someone is there, kiss them
Even if you both have dragon breath!

Pick your outfit by the colors of your mood
Go outside barefoot if it's not too cold
And salute the sun.
Listen for birds
Feel the Mother underfoot
Always supporting you.

Say thank you to the Universe
That you are alive.
Take your medicine!
Expect to fix your own breakfast
And do it up right.

Get some chores out of the way
Annoying, but you will feel better.
Take breaks for conscious breathing
Do some things that feed your soul
Create something
Listen to music and also sing.

Pick some basil and cherry tomatoes
Take a nap
Make love if possible
Wake ready for the late sunset
Drive towards water
Walk or meditate.

Get the mail at 10 pm
Breathe and pray
Watch a movie
Read yourself to sleep.

JOY

Joy comes like a sunbeam
Comes shining into my bedroom
At dawn, tapping on my weary
Eyelids, whispering you have
Another day... your life did not bleed away.
Get up, please, never mind those painful knees.

I hobble out my door as birds greet the sun,
The kind grass is under me, I raise my arms
In one motion of instinctive praise.
There is nothing wrong with the day
And nothing wrong with suffering,
But joy is also here to stay!

IF I TOLD
THE TRUTH

ANOTHER WINTER

Sometime, when the river is ice, ask me
If my warm blood has iced as well, if
My dreams sleep like small fish, far beneath
The surfaces I walk on, the thick, cold surfaces
That seem to hold my weight, but could crack at random,
Spilling my life into black water.

Ask me how the darkness calls to me
With a kind of galactic whistling
How the sparkling snow in moonlight
Invites me to lie down and never rise.
Ask me if I remember what I came here to do.

Sometime, when even eagles shiver in their nests, when
Branches snap and fall
On hard ground, ask me where I go
When I am not with you.
Maybe I will mention the midnight crossroads
Where pale-eyed hounds snap and bawl,
And shadows more solid than darkness rise up,
Guide me to a land so far I won't be sending you
A postcard.

Sometime, when February seems like a mental illness
That can't be solved by pill or light box,
Ask me if I regret a single thing, and I will say nothing.
If you look closely, you will see how
Pain has etched me, how my body is a road map
Of everywhere I have been.

Sometime, when the sky is tarnished
Pewter, and the North wind cries in the waste places,
Stalks the trembling houses like a terrible giant,
Ask me if I believe in God's plan for my life
I will say, "There is no god. There is no plan."

WHAT MAKES ME "ME"?

It must be my big belly and
All its longings, it must be that
Womb wisdom rising, those naughty nipples,
That solar power in my solar plexus. It must be
The indigo states of consciousness lit
With diamond sparks, the wounds, the hallucinations.

It must be my busy hands, my aching body
My patience and frustration. It must be heart
Drumming, the journey that flows down
Every river and shows no signs of ending.

It must be the beautiful faces I look into
With love and praise, the intersections
Of my words with others' lives and words, the
Love exchanged, limitless. It must be the music
Inner and outer, the Islands of Awareness, then
The sinking down again into that inky sea....

It must be waterfalls singing to my spirit
Grandchildren holding me as I hold space for them
It must have been my stubborn mule marriage, my stubborn
Nature. It must be the fact that if you kiss me
I will not forget it.

Yet I know I am just
A temporary arrangement of energy, an actress
In the sacred play before returning to the source
For refreshments. My very atoms will be shuffled,
Repurposed... I will hang out in the unknown bardos,
Still deluded enough by energy monsters
To follow the dark red light— right back
Into incarnation, and curiously, I don't mind.

CHANNELED POEM

I am a flame of fire, blazing
With passionate love
I am a spark of light
Illuminating the deepest truth
I am the energy of the Big Bang
Still expanding outwards
Expressing the life of the cosmos
With my tiny spark
Dancing the dance of life
On the atomic stage
I am blue light deep in winter woods
Beckoning the lost and weary
The comfort of the campfire
With coffee and pancakes
Welcoming human and animal alike
I am the candle by the mirror
In the dark room
That allows you to see your ancestors
Parading through your own face.
I am the light of wisdom in the heart space
Always glowing and available
I am the vestal virgin
Tending the fire that must never go out
I am the mother who blazes with love
For her children, the one who will protect them
Against all odds.
I am the spooky Crone at the crossroads.
Only the light of the waning moon
Illuminates my eyes and the eyes of my hounds.
I am the light that nurtures crops
I am the sunspots acting up
And ruining everyone's plans
I am the day, I am high noon
Because of me, nearly everyone can see!

CHANNELED POEM 2

My heart is a field—
A field of earth
Planted with the seeds of spirit
Watered by an ocean of tears
Nurtured by the morning sun
Sprouting in the mystery of moonlight.

I am green corn growing—
My roots cling fast to the Mother
My bodies dance with wind and Father Sky
I am ripening, bursting.

I am yellow corn in the dawn light
I am red corn in the house of summer
I am blue corn bowing to Thunder beings
I am white corn in the north.

My milky kernels feed the villages
I feed the nations of birds
Four-footeds feed on me,
I nurture body and spirit of the human tribes.

My heart is a fallow field
With broken stalks, rustling with mice
Brown, sepia, receptive as a valley
I wait for the seasons of the spirit.

UNTITLED

The frantic beggar's empty purse—
Filled with greatest
Effort, spent again without a pause
I empty, I fill—
My heart is a puzzle with
One piece missing
I give it almost whole, a
Damaged present from the Goodwill
Then panic— what's left for me?
Frantically, I fill my holes
And
The heavier I get,
The more I leak

AM

I am life and death, life and breath
Waves of the sea flowing through me
Children grow, people come and go
There's everything to know and everywhere to go
And then you have to let it all go
Let it all go, back to the source.

I am sight and sound, colors all around
Dizzy dancing prairie grass
Snake that's graceful on the path
Shifting shapes, eating grapes
Sending out a telegram... but then
You have to let it all go.

I am a mother bear, a lioness in her lair
I can fight my battles, shake the shaman rattles
I can walk among the wounded
Touching them with healing care
I am energy, powerful, woman full of blood
I can slog a thousand miles through the mud,
Then make breakfast, but you know
Sooner or later, I have to let it all go.

I am an artist, I know where to look
I am a writer working on a book
I love the music, I love to make the scene
I love community life, I want to be seen.
But when the party's over and I went back to my lover
I looked into his eyes and had to realize
One of these days he will have to let it go.

Death is walking in the yard; death is breathing very hard
Down my mortal neck
And the wreck of my body sizes down my days
And brings me to my knees, and to the
Divine.

I say please, please, don't let it be me, not this time
Please just let me be— I love it here, you see?
And I live to breathe another day
Old death smiles and fades away
But as I am walking in the yard
Doing my best to work so hard
And earn my keep before I sleep
I see a baby bird, fallen from the nest
And gone to its eternal rest, and I know
One of these days, I have to let it all go...
I'm going to let it all go.

IF I TOLD THE TRUTH

The whole truth, and nothing but
I think I would have to be at home
A part of my truth is that a part of me
Actively loves to be alone.
So why don't I have my true and final say
Let the chips fall
Let the full complement of shit
Hit the proverbial fan?
And if everyone backs away from me
As if I am a leper
If my truth hits them between the eyes
Or slides between their ribs like a knife?
Or if they reject it and it runs down their bodies
Onto the floor? Like a gob of something
Why, what then?

If I told the truth
It would be so complicated
It might take a lifetime to tell
Or maybe it would be so simple
A powerful release, satori!
I know from bitter experience that few
People in my life want the entire story
Especially not those closest... they want
Consistency, reassurance; they want me in a role
Or they want a piece of me, not the whole package!

I am not what anyone wants me to be
I am not the same person ALL the time!
I am lazy and selfish, an impractical dreamer.
I am naughty and capricious and my Libra scales
Swing wildly when I try to make my mind up.
I am a bundle of contradictions, a complicated human.

I want both/and but usually have to settle
For either/or. But I never give up on both/and!
Both family and solitude
Both men and women

Both spiritual and sensual
Both responsible and care free
Both hermetic and adventurous
Open to all love, all the time.
Not capable of living up to my own ideals.
Suspicious of all ideals, aspire to be vegetarian
And still get lured to meat
Both meditate and smoke pot... this list could go on
If I told the whole truth, I would probably be sorry!

UNTITLED

How deep into night can one travel?
How deep can we snuggle
in a small nest of animal warmth,
surrounded by the vast impersonal chill
of a starlit sky, the blank white earth?

How far behind can we leave our bodies
as we dream, fly, and swim
in the Winter midnight?

Bear in her cave, turning
in familiar fetid darkness, dreams
of digging her medicine plants in dripping woodlands
feels the warmth inside her,
her mother's work not done.

WHAT SAVES ME

Lately it's been hard; I don't feel saved— I'm all used up, I am brittle
   as a milkweed pod
With all the fluff gone right into my brain.
I'm down the drain and swirling in a pile of soapy hair
And wet despair, it is difficult to share
What it is that holds a hand out, helps me up
And keeps me slogging on.
I am so gone past religion
Though I hold on to my mantra like a rosary of words
OM TARA TU TARA TU RE SO HA
Carries me into darkness, into the sparkling void
Of no-self, hums me to sleep, or lets me travel deep
Beneath the surface of this crazy life
Where I have held my hands
To the lit candles of lovers,
Looked and looked and looked at books
Lost myself in the bright colors of music
I've wandered in the lower world in a state of trance
Visited the embodied stories of the mystic world of dance.
When I am smart, I lose myself and save myself in the magic
Trick of art. But really there is no escape, no saving grace
Just life and pain, joy and wonder
Fear, darkness, and light.

MY HEART IS FULL AGAIN

My heart is full and sore, with painful
Thumping
Like it's been run over with a truck,
Squished out blood and gore
And yet it is my karmic luck:
It heals itself and goes on pumping.

My heart is full of sorrow
For the Ferris Wheel we're on
The illusions so thick they're crawling
Over my skin, I hold so many people
In that tiny heart space
Secret tears are shed for them
I pray to Goddess to keep them safe.

My heart is battered by the tides
Of politics and war— it hurts to know that
Innocents are wounded to the core, without
A home, without a voice, without
A grocery store.
It hurts that I can't reach out to them
Bring comfort, food, and joy
I can't protect my very own
Much less these girls and boys.

My heart is full with knowing
This life we know is slowly ending
Ecosystems delicate dance
Are on the edge and sending messages for help,
Messages for healing.
Icebergs melt, the sun beats down
You know just what I am feeling
My heart is full of joy as well: it wells up
All the time; I see past all illusions
And ultimately, everything is fine.

WHAT MATTERS

I have my own ideas
But I wish I truly knew
In some definitive way
What matters to whom?
To me personally
To my descendants, to the oceans,
To the children of the world?
What matters to justice, to balance
To peace and reasonable prosperity?
What matters to the universe?
To the void from which all form springs?
And who am I anyway?
I have a voice, a point of view
I passionately believe and make my voice heard
Yet an inner voice says "What do you
Really know? What I think I know
Is that evolution and devolution
Go on together, inseparable as Yin-Yang
That forms come and go, energy
Seems infinite
Humans are infinitely precious
Yet not as special as we think,
One more genetic experiment
I like to think that Gaia can shake Herself
Free of us if we don't work out
What matters to shivering human self
Is the future suffering of all the children.

UNTITLED

Life cuts me where I touch it, evades
My fervent grasp and shatters beyond control
Then is whole.
When all the honey was licked off the moon
It became a crisp white
Wafer and sailed through the night.
I pursued it, eager for a bite
I ate the moon
I ate the world
Then swallowed my pride
Now it cuts me
From inside
I need to spew
Out all that earth, that bitter
Rind of love-fruit gone sour
I need to scour
My mirrors
Reflecting guilt, greed, shame.
I need to hear that name
That says
Pure beautiful self
Is not cut
Is not touched.

I DON'T KNOW WHY I PULLED THIS CARD

Twice in tarot readings: the Nine of Swords.
In every life a day comes, or a night
Things happen that don't seem right,
A tragedy, catastrophe, Death visits, or the fear of Death
Draws near and the Mind cannot process,
The Heart cannot bear. One looks for escape (which is nowhere)
Swords surround you, beautiful and deadly
You may have to use them— and even if you craft
Your own escape, you will not get away without scars.

AUTOBIOGRAPHY

8   Fat

9   Fatter

10   Menarche

11   Moving across the city

12   Friends

13   Junior high

14   Books and art

15   Books and art and theater

16   Books and art, theater and choir

17   Friends and singing(beatnik!)

18   Freedom (college)

19   Misfit, trying to lose my virginity

20   Sex and psychedelics, amazing rock music, toured Europe for a whole summer!

21   Drop-out college girl

22   Pregnant

23   Married, working the midnight shift for IRS in Kansas City

24   Baby girl!

24   Hippie travels

27   Baby girl 2

28   Marital discord

29   See 28

30   Still fighting

31   Still fighting

32   Baby girl 3

33   Still married, I had a crush

34   As above

35   Poverty

36   Poverty

37   Poverty

38   Fighting

39   Fighting

40   Poverty

41   Fighting

43	Working
44	Working
45	Working
46	Working
47	Acknowledging my paganism
48	Peri-menopause
49	I am so freaking hot!
50	Menopause, thank GODDESS
51	Working
52	Younger kids misbehaving
53	Ditto
54	Ditto
55	Ditto
56	Ditto
57	Kids in counseling, beginning to settle
58	Hubby and I in counseling, learning how to fight fair
59	Kids settling down, kids moving out
60	Grandsons (In Portland, OR) and granddaughters in Lawrence
61	Marital harmony
62	Ditto, travel and adventure
63	Yup, travel
64	Ditto
65	Travel, but physical problems
66	Still traveling, but it is getting harder for my old man each year
67	Life is slowing a bit, lots of medical trauma/drama
68	We get along incredibly well
69	Started noticing I have physical problems, also help with his
70	Still taking care of our ancient house and garden, more slowly
71	Husband has many ER visits, always at night, and needs a lot of care... he has good doctors. Once in a while I lose a gall bladder or take stupid falls, but I bounce back.
72	We had grown so close that it was amazing, he was sicker
73	Husband dies (last December)
74	I am still here...I miss him so much... and that is my story for now.
75	I did not get to throw in all the grandkids... three boys, two girls!

HOW I WANT TO LIVE MY LIFE

I know I want to be outside,
Serenaded by bird song
Shaded beneath sister trees
Listening to messages whispered by wind.
I know I want to lie, bare and blissed
On Earth Mama, sob my sorrow
Take Her massive comfort into me,
Listen to her heart, listen to my heart
Beating on for no reason.
I know I want to slip into green or blue water
Float on my back like otter
Watch storm clouds gather
Let myself be loose
I know I want to be big Mama
Surrounded by loved ones as I offer a feast
Prepared by my own hands, healthy glowing
Food just harvested, and I say "eat, eat!"
I know I always wanted to lie
Beside you, husband, not every night
But over and over finding your mouth with mine
In the dark, feel your pulse
Faint or flooding beneath my searching fingers.
I want to open wider to the world
Of senses and beyond
Open to the rich ground of myth and ritual
Open to the monsters, within and without—
Encounter them with love and embrace them
As my own, I want to love all children
As dearly as my own, and learn from every one
I want to love... life, myself, others, spirit— deeply
And without limiting my options. I want to sing
I want to drum and hear my voice rise up
To blend with others harmony—
I want to look into the eyes of my friends
Let them see me, let them feel all the love that is there.
I want to praise this wonderful mystery of life.
I want to celebrate, again and again.

TWO SPIRIT

I am a woman, greeted the moon
With forty years of red tides
I have been penetrated, pierced through
Babies came through me. I have suckled
And supported so many... I've taught children
To sing and fight fair, joined them in
In their joys. My heart is the heart
Of the wild Mother that speaks to plants
And listens... everything is sacred, everything
Hums to me. I am Willendorf woman
Soft fat comforter... I probably baked
Your birthday cake... how then to speak
Of the man in me (that spot of yang in my yen)
I barely understand myself
How that delicate balance can lead to health
Or madness, sometimes on the same day.
Whiskers sprouted in my fifties
My feet would only fit men's shoes
As for male and female bodies
As an artist I don't have to choose.
Some mornings the mirror shows
The stern red visage of my father
I felt myself hardening into a new
Configuration. My tears dry up
And heart beats a sullen warrior beat
Mouth fills with lava, and I could cheat
At cards, draw a knife, or leave you... temporarily.
I must be in the world then
And flee my feathered nest
Don't stop me or I'll hurt you
Even though I love you best.
I'm going on a quest to visit my shadow
To know myself without boundaries.

A GOOD TIME TO START SOMETHING NEW

Marooned on a small island of self-doubt
In my 55th year
Hobbled by old pain
And a marriage
Filled with cups of tea and gloomy silences.
My children struggling
Wrestling with their karma
While I sit stark awake
In four A.M. computer light
Praying to the Goddess
Or playing Thieves and Kings
Ideas dropping from the sieve of my brain
A light and steady rain
This ruined body flinching at
So many dead around me
Whispering and rustling—
So many loves gone forever.
Outside the leaves ready themselves
To spring out green from the dead, gray branches
If there ever was a time, it's now
"A good time to start something new"

CHANGE THE WORLD

I am leaving
I lied to you
I betrayed you
I am pregnant
I have another lover
I enlisted!
These are only a few
of the potent minutes that chew
up reality and spit it out!

WHAT I HEAR IN SILENCE

Whether it's going to sleep
Or formal meditation
It's always the same
First, I hear my breath
Go in and out, gradually quieting.

If my eyes are closed
I see an inner firmament,
Dark and in motion
With intricate ever-changing
Patterns of the most subtle light...

As I settle into the silence
I hear the sounds of summer insects,
A chorus of crickets and locusts
Directly inside my head
As I listen, an overtone arises
Very high and very faint
Like celestial bells
Like the music Radha
Played on her finger cymbals
To entice Krishna her love.

DISEQUILIBRIUM

I am so off-balance
From my one gimpy leg
From knees that cry for mercy
From the onrush of reality
That seldom lets up.

I limp to the bathroom
Cook and bake from a walker
Go downtown with a cane.
On good days
I fill a few big pots with plants
Then have to rest my aching back,
My crooked spine
Or I lie on the ground in the garden
To pull weeds
And earth takes my sorrow
Comforts me with herbs and iris.

The moon goes through
Many intense cycles
There is much drama,
Little silence.
She shows many things
In her dark phase
In the darkness of my dreams.
Makes me second-guess myself
Falter, shut down
Come back, return.

My Libra scales
Are never at rest
Long enough to experience peace
(As a dimension that unrolls in time).
The world pushes me, hard
My body is valiant and suffering
There are worries and frustration.
Two people with health issues
The sex takes a hit
As well.

SHE SAID, I SAID

She said: "I've been so."
I said "I know what you mean, I've
Had such a –" She said "God, it's been so hard
I mean to tell you when I—"
I said: "It is terrible
When I worry so," and she said:
"It's hard on me, it never ends.
I thought it would be better when?" I said
"The suffering never seems to end."
She said "I will always, and if only—"
I said "Let's just be enlightened.
Why wait any longer, since things
Are always what they are?" She said
"But how, and dare we?"
I said "Let's just do it now."
There was nothing else to say.

STILL TIME

I know there is still time
To luxuriate in the totality of the moment

Really this is all we have
But life offers it endlessly
Revealing vistas of memory and chance
Rare random awareness,
Exquisite pain, melting beauty
More love than we can possibly know

I know there is time
For everything
When we lose our passionate attachment
To the particular way
We think it should be
And open like our baby's mouth
Trusting the rich milk of the Mother
Trusting the deep well
At the bottom of our souls

I know there is time
For thirst to be quenched
And every hunger sated
We come home to a feast
And hear those most-loved voices
Saying "All is forgiven."

A RECIPE FOR HAPPINESS

First, you have to love yourself
You may disapprove your bad habits
But you need to know that you are, well, wonderful!
Second, be humble and don't
Take yourself too seriously.
Acknowledge your own faults
And be ready to shoulder the blame
When you make costly mistakes.
Don't rush into marriage
Even if a baby is involved
Understand this person deeply
And reveal your own underbelly.
If you do tie the knot, understand
This is a journey of a lifetime!
Do your utmost to make it work
Be responsible and clear headed
Remember that neither alcohol or drugs
Are likely to improve your situation.
Alone or together
Know that you are here and now
For a reason. Sooner or later
You will know what it is.
Be as good as you can, and kind!
Forgive mistakes, your own and others
Enjoy your life, all of it
Allow yourself gratitude
Whether or not you believe in God, you can
Believe in the universe, since you
Are a conscious part of it.
Wonder at the beauty and awe of your life
And notice all that is around you—
The simple satisfactions go a long way.
Stop worrying so much, just be
A great person— spouse, parent, friend
You will survive as long as you are supposed to be here.
Don't fear death, it is part of the cycle.

RETURN OF LIGHT

You have no idea
How I crave you
Chill starlit reality
On hot nights in August
On days in July
When the sun hangs too long
In the sullen, hazy sky.

The fertile darkness is my shaman,
My muse
I need to be warm, of course
Under the comforter
Or in the bearskin.

My eyes relax
Reality the same sparkling void
Whether my lids are closed
Or open.

My breath becomes huge,
Self-conscious.
Then peaceful.

Body relaxes and surrenders
It is my time being
What I return to
When not misled by ego and form.

I am vast, no different
From this darkness,
Not pretty or smart, bored or sad.

From this spaciousness straight to sleep
And the dreams come like snow
Thick, fast, almost comprehensible.

Voices speak inside me
Awake! Awake!

ABOUT THE WAR

Snow falls gently through quiet purple air
As falling sun pulls light from yet another day
Blackbirds brood and squawk themselves to cold sleep
And squirrels dream of hoarded treasure in their holes.
Indoors, families huddle over steaming soup and break
Or kneel to pray for the USA.
Snow falls with grace in the fragile places
Where we live, and hope to carve our little lives
While all that we had hoped for, all we thought was ours
Flees away on madmen's schemes and children's screams.
Snow falls innocent and beautiful over the ruined
Landscape of our dreams
Our hopes for wisdom were put on permanent hold
As bloody butchers hack the world to pieces,
Devour it raw and bleeding.

IMPERMEABLE

I feel my heart but cannot hear it
A small chamber of pain and bliss
Radiation from the chest—
Flooding the brain, flooding the eyes
Sending pulsations thrilling
Through the rivers of my blood.

I am, I love, I ache
For the deceptively fragile body
Of creation
And its simultaneous destruction
For the unselfish plants
And doomed animals
For the humans who only want to live
For the humans who only want to kill
For the children already living
In their bewildering new world,
Not knowing what they have
Or what they are missing.

I feel my heart but cannot hear it
Silent love, silent pain
Something to lose
Something to gain
This is the human condition
Floating in the soup of it all
Love forms
Helpless as a fat little meatball.

SHADOW

My shadow hides in darkness
Sunlight brings it out
Doing its snaky dance in front of me
As I walk— or behind me
Where others can see it and I cannot
My shadow is rich with knowledge; I need
Its fertile darkness which holds so many keys
To living well, living my authentic life.

It is the missing piece, the numinous secret
The worst nightmare, the hopes that never
Found their voice.
I have a little shadow
It goes in and out with me
I get more and more acquainted
As I pile up history.

My shadow is a pagan
My shadow is the body
My shadow goes a-begging.
My shadow is
So naughty!
Yet I have learned to visit shadow realms.
Listen to the whispers and the moans, hear the voices
Of the dead; be not afraid when they shake their bones!

My shadow is the half of me, half that most folks
Never see; my strengths and weaknesses tangled
Together, neurosis, mistakes, nefarious weather.
Creativity, courage, far-seeing, compassion
Contradictions, restrictions, half-truth fictions.
Do you happen to have one too?

ADVENTURE

What could be a bigger adventure
Than life itself? First, the womb
And darkness
The peaceful unknowing
Floating in sensation
Effortlessly fed by the pulsating umbilical
Our chakras like flower beds
Waiting to unfold.
Then that restless day or night
When we sense changes are afoot
We shift and elbow, suck our fetal thumbs
And feel the earthquake beginning
Undulating, groaning,
Pushing us into unbearable light
If we are lucky our early adventures are benign
First taste of banana, blissful access
To the breast.... warm baths and siblings singing
A green yard with birds and trees, friendly
Puppies—then we start to school and
Adventures get bigger, the joy of letters and numbers!
Paint and puzzles and playing cymbals
In the rhythm band. Then there are new bullies
On the playground, friends becoming enemies
On the walk home, and the whispers on the fire escape
('And he puts his... you-know into your wee-wee
OH NO HE DOESN'T, you liar! ...) but we sense the
Mysteries ahead. The stakes keep getting higher
We become adults with decisions to make
And every one opens a door into
An altered reality... that never stops changing
Changing, calling, challenging
When we finally slow down
Start to look forward to the weary womb darkness
Of sleep... we turn the corner
To the deepest adventure left...
Dying, death, rebirth!

WHAT THE HEART WANTS

Much more than there is time for, given
Any one life, this heart, steadily beating
And hungry for times and places
All manner of stories stretching back
To prehistory, cave stories by flickering light
Strange chants of boatmen on the Nile
Encountering bare-breasted goddesses in Crete
As the young wasp-waisted and black-curled girls and boys leap over
    bulls.

This heart wants many lives.
In this time, multiple stories layering and connecting
Sewing together quilts of experience, gleaning
Gold from the stream of daily life, mining for deep emotions
Always learning, connecting, expanding.

This heart wants more love, given and taken, as much as it
Could hold, never-ending streams of awareness gushing
From peaks of experience, gathering force as it hails through
The Headlands, becoming calm in the plains of Middle age.

This heart craves richness, infinity, dark skies—
With distant points of light, fires burning on
Into the night.
Music, death, births, sex.
This little heart wants too much joy. NOT NOW.

If not now, then more and more, it seems like NEVER.
I lie awake, raking the embers of the past, reviewing my bucket list.
One never knows for sure— as long as we are alive,
Our life is still loading— but I can say with certainty the ME of now,
    this persona will never return to Crete, never make it to Barcelona.

I'll worship the Goddess here at home but never
Take the Goddess tour of the British Isles.
I'll never ride a bicycle as I did so happily growing up.
I'll never make it to New Zealand. Enough!

If "when" is removed from the equation, I still have "now"
And in a moment now again, and now again.
My "when" is an ongoing "now!"
I realize this is all I can really grasp.
If not when, I'll live in the present, though evil kings presently burden
  the Earth.
And the present will richly reward me with an ordinary life of love
  and sorrow, kisses and spats, moments of true magic.

There is a reason they call the Present a gift!

MY WORK IS LOVING

No more, no less
Often an uphill battle
Given the whole of the human
Condition, hardest of course
Is loving the self
Looking in mirrors all around you
At your own grave imperfections
Your old-lady whiskers, fat belly
Completely unacceptable fantasies
Your mistakes and mishaps surrounding
You like a gray mist

But a day comes when you look in
Not out, and see your own radiant self
Pure as any other and with tears and joy
You forgive yourself, deeply accept yourself
And suddenly become a channel, a Vessel
That love can effortlessly pass through

My work is loving, only judgment gets in the way
My art, my writing go through the intricate
Rituals of each day but really there is nothing
Nothing left to do, nowhere to be, except here— Now!
Sending and receiving, pulsing with awareness
Of our true nature here on earth, our destiny
What we can give back to creation
Every day!

I AM STILL HERE. SEND WATER!

Beating my drum, I arouse the Cosmos
Announcing again and again:
"I am still here. Send water!"
My thirsty buds need tender mercy
To open their scented beauty to the sky.

MY LIFE

My life, my dearest life
Hold on to me
I am not ready to go.
So much of me is history
So many stories whisper mystery
Why, O why, leave beloveds aside
When you can still hold them at your side?
When family goes the extra miles,
When friends grab my arm and guide me
For a while, I want to see what happens next.

I know my generation is planning its burial
Most of us are becoming mercurial; will we come
Back as ghosts, or television hosts?
My life is unpredictable and scary— I have to do
What the doctor says and bide by the pills that
May help... or eat fat-free chicken and a daily
Dose of kelp?

I remember how my husband
Began to trip and fall for no apparent reason
Except cold snow in the slippery season.
He got on a ladder to reach a shelf— he had not
Informed me to come and help, and then it was
Too late... he died peaceably although his words were gone.

Now new years have passed— we all get older, more frightened,
Maybe bolder. Hold onto me a little until
I cannot write or speak, then let me go. I'm curious, you know. Most
    of all I will do my best to let him know, and you as well.
I loved all of you. I loved you— I really, truly loved you!

CALLING SPIRITS

KUAN YIN

The Goddess sent me
Green and pink energy today
Exquisite as roses
On stems of light

Her arrows painlessly pierced
My breast to heal me
She told me to learn
To feel from my womb
Before it's too late

Goddess knows
I am a desperate woman
Stumbling through life
The Fool of the tarot
And yet she blesses me
With monarch, hawk, and crow

Blessed me with people
Children, song...
Still, I am a desperate woman
One who is bleeding
For much too long

Today I prayed
The Compassionate One
Entered my head
Brought me dazzling electrical fields
In the fabulous hyperspace
Inside my eyes
Played flute songs directly on my nerves

Bathed in bliss, yet
I beg as a baby
For her breasts, her fierce embrace

A PRAYER FOR KALI

Oh Kali, black mother
I do not fully understand you
But your turbulent dance
Is occurring in my heart
Whether I like it or not...

You, the merciful, who destroys
Old forms, old pain
And drinks the blood of demons
Striking them down with wrath
You, the milk-filled mother
Giving birth to all creation
Snakes and animals, humans
And demigods.

Wriggling out of your womb
In a constant stream... you with the necklace
Of heads, and all of them smiling
Oh Kali, black mother
Dance your terrible, wonderful dance
Let the earth return to primal ecstasy!

HEALER

Small intense being
Enters my private space
Radiant as a speckled egg
With a tiny sun inside her...
Stepping quickly to drum
And didgeridoo
She reverently lifts a prayer feather
Mutters soft prayers at my altar
As her bones hollow out,
She scrubs herself empty
Then brushes my aura
Clear of snarls
The mundane bedroom
Fills with eagle spirit
My numb heart warms
As she grounds me
 With smoky quartz
Places crystal over my heart
Puts a stone on my aching belly
Now we are floating together
Into dreamtime
She is using my earth want
To stroke my skin
My nipples are hard
But I am soft and calm
Her fingers coax knots from my body
And the scents of lavender and thyme
Mix with chanting
And I could swear my room
Is full of wings and feathers

MOTHER TONGUE

I spoke your tongue of old, Mother
In the hot Babylonian temple
When I became an aspect of the Goddess
And received strange men
In stone rooms filled with fragrant resins
They worshiped my source
With their eager phalluses
I spoke the language of your serpents
And cartwheeled over bull's backs
Learned the cadence of your songs and spells

In the middle days, my family whispered secrets
Ways to be in the dangerous world
Ways of power and beauty
I knew your tongue
But I had to hide it
The women and children saw Your glow in me
Came to me secretly
I spoke your tongue
In a world divided into devils and angels
Frightened souls saw evil everywhere
Mother, I speak your tongue

In my crazy new world
The birds taught me
The trees and wind speak to me
A glance, a sunbeam
Rabbit meadows in moonlight
The nacreous light
Of sunset on the water
I walk barefoot upon you, grow roots,
Feed, drink— nowadays I grow old
Forget the words, but not the giant pulsing
Of your fiery core

GODDESS HEAR MY PRAYER

Come near me and enter my heart
Let me be empty, and filled with
Your presence. Let me be a vessel that
Your energy may flow through. Look out
From my eyes and inform my seeing.
Let me be empty so I can be filled with your love.

Goddess who hears the cries and prayers of the world,
Who manifests over and over as compassionate
Wisdom, lend me your wisdom. Let it pour through
This faulty vessel, so that I may be worthy
Of this human incarnation. Let me be
Strong enough to love what I am given, rather than what
I fantasize. Give me the patience to endure
My circumstances, and sometimes transcend them.

Bless my hands and my eyes, bless my body and my days.
Give me, please, abundance so that I
Can share love abundantly, stand up for the earth,
Stand up for peace and justice.
Stand up for children, always.
Give me fortitude to be fair witness to my friends and neighbors,
The courage to speak the truth.

I love you without limit, your beauty makes me swoon, and
Most of all, dearest Goddess who infuses me with her
Divine spark, please let me see you, so that I
Do not lose hope. So mote it be.

WHEN YOU REACH THE BOTTOM, GO DEEPER!

You have always dreamed
That under the ocean
Was another ocean, even more magical
Uproot some rocks,
Kick through some muck, dig sand like a maniac
While your oxygen lasts.

The hole is deeper— keep going! Keep going!
There is nowhere to go except down—
And first you feel it, then you see the strange, young
Light of a new world
Into which you drop, head first, a newborn
In the same old body... or— wait, wait!
Why are you not drowning?
Your gills are working
Just fine.

LOVE AND ATTACHMENT

Love is the energy that drives
the Universe at the most fundamental level.
The lesson of becoming a Crone is to love
with all your might, give everything you are capable
of giving. Burn brightly. Accept the people and situations
You are given, see them clearly and do everything you can
To use the energy of unconditional love in each relationship
and situation!

Oddly, this works much better when you are
fundamentally unattached to the outcome. If it turns out
not fair, whether or not your efforts are seen clearly or acknowledged,
you learn to rest in the knowledge that you will get what you need,
and that you did your personal best.

Native Americans are so right on in acknowledging that after
    menopause,
a woman is no longer just for her family. As a Crone, we have
    somewhat more leisure—
our kids have grown, we retire at some point, we become community
            gatekeepers
in whatever capacity and we learn to turn our consciences inward,
dream and scheme for seven generations!
Some things we become better at doing, even as our physical
    capacities drain.

CALLING SPIRITS

By the triple power of three times three
I call the host of winged spirits to me!

Fly from the East, ye bringers of dawn light
Fire-dance from South, ye spirits of delight
Out of the West swim, Undines watery
From crystalline North, old spirits that wise be.

With salt and smoke I make a circle of light—
Spirits bring power to help me tonight.
Ancestor Spirits, I ask help from thee
Animal totems wherever you be,
Come to my circle, if not to my sight
Help me raise power if ye think it right.

To all spirit beings, hail and well-met
Thank you for coming, I am in your debt.

ME AND KALI

I asked Kali if
she had plans for me
and did they involve
my death.
And She said, "Yes."

I asked Her if She meant
sooner or later.
And She said,
"Don't worry about that.
You'll be around just as long
as need be."

I asked Kali
would I be reborn.
She rolled Her eyes
and did Her awesome dance
of destruction and creation
as I watched.

And She said:
"All that is old and outworn
I will destroy.
I will dance on the bones
of greed and war.
I will take your body
when you don't need it anymore."
She said, "I will make a path
for the new, and
all things will be recycled."

I asked Kali,
"But what about me?
Will I still be here then?"
And She said, "Woman,
You just don't get it."

MEETING AT THE CROSSROADS

Has to be midnight
Has to be dark moon, it is
Going to meet your fate soon
Walking to the crossroads
Carrying your heavy loads
This is the life you have loved and made
It is going to change, don't be afraid!

Closer to the crossroads, the clouds
Are closing in; you wonder why you're
Daring this, what's going to begin?

Hear the howling of Her hounds
And know you're very near
She is coming here to meet with you
This Crone you love and fear.
Some do call her Hecate, others say
"The Crone." She's beautiful!
And ancient, magical to the bone!

She has made a little campfire, Her dogs
Have settled down. She looks at you with wisdom eyes, and suddenly
You've found answers to your questions, the ones
That hurt your heart; she takes you in her bony arms
And there, YOU fall apart. She puts you back
Together, whispers to your brain.

Hecate, oh Hecate! I have everything to lose or
Everything to gain.
By the triple power of three times three,
Hecate, by three times three,
Shine your sacred light on me!

HOMAGE TO THOMAS MERTON

In the four quarters of the world, the wind is still
At the bottom of breath, there is a pause
That speaks of death. Deep silence is felt
Filled with the ancient sorrow of all the human race
Has lost, the wind holds its peace, and clouds pause
In their ceaseless travels...
This is the stillness that
All of us have longed for, the psalm not uttered.
Ten thousand eons seem to pass, without comment
Yet this communion continues, deeper than words.
Then, with a visceral, subsonic scream
Into the space that the lightning bolt vacated.
Everyone fills their lungs
With unspeakable gratitude, and a small
Breeze, quiet as a sigh, nudges
The clouds on across the sky.

HALLOWEEN!

Halloween!
All Hallows' Eve
Samhain...
Night between the equinox and solstice
Darkness of the old year,
Darker still ahead of us.

The veil between the worlds
Grows thin
The veil may let things out
And let things in.
The present is a magic lighted door
Dim past behind us
Freaky future in front of us.
The present is a magic lighted door
Enter it
You are always entering it
To encounter the beyond
And at midnight tonight
The veil between the astral
And the material
Will be nothing.
You may step through if you choose
And know this universe in a new way.

But even if you don't
There are others who chose to
Come here, to your reality
Spirits of the dead
Who wish to be honored
Waiting for flowers or a plate of food
Waiting to hear a word of
Themselves, a loving thought
Some are confused or angry
Speak to them, don't be afraid
Wish them well, wish them rebirth
Light incense
And let your prayers rise
To God or Goddess.

Tonight is the night
High holy day
For pagans
A time when, for a brief moment,
All is possible.

Halloween
Playful, joyful, scary, sexual
A time for all children
Old and young,
But don't go out late
In the woods tonight
The wild hunt may be riding.
Do not presume they are gone!
Hecate will be at the crossroads
With her baying hounds.

In this Scorpio
Dark-of-the-moon night
Do you dare
To face her?
It's just possible
That Baron Samedi
Is out there too.
Would you let yourself be
Ridden by the Loa?
Would you be his spirit horse?

Halloween!
All Hallows' Eve
Samhain...
The veil between the world is thin
And only the season's last marigold's
Glimmering in the darkness
Hold the memory of the sun's rays.

HEAR ME, O WOMEN

I am the Caillach
I am the Crone
I love to be alone
I dance in just My bones
I meditate on My throne.

Everything you are
I have been
I am the Goddess of bitter and sweet, the baby
Who lived and the one who died
The runaway child,
The strong maiden oppressed.

I have been beaten, raped, kidnapped
I have lost untold lives, fighting
For My freedom
I have burned as a witch
For healing My people
Been jailed for speaking up, for showing up.

I have sadly aborted babies,
I have had too many children and
Not enough children
I have lost children and found them
I have been the abused wife, also
The poisoner, the crafty one, who
Tricks Her way among the dangers
I have had too many lovers to count, My dears,
Only one was and is a true partner.

I have loved women as well as men
And been persecuted for that as well.
I have been the Maiden, the Mother, the Grandmother
The Great-Grandmother,
I have been the Queen and the Sacred Prostitute, worshiped as Astarte
In My temple. Holy! Holy!

I have been the Mother of tribes
I was there when the men destroyed our icons and razed our temples,
When the Mother was forgotten and the sky-god ruled it all.

Hear me, My women!
Do not despair
I am the Goddess of ecstasy
Every death leads to rebirth
The ego is nothing, a gadfly!
We are divine light at the core.

I have had such joy
Of the living earth!
Each of us is the center of the universe
I have danced with stars
I have danced with the Moon, delirious
Rode the turning wheel of fate, rode horses, rode
Men— oh yes, I am as human and divine as you are!

Yet these days, I don't stay in my body all the time
I'm in and out of form, you know?
It's easier to get around that way.
These days, I'm ancient, My breasts
Hang, half empty bags, no moisture
Left between My legs.
I sleep alone. My bones made of stone,
My chestnut hair is snow;
There is nowhere left to go.

Hear Me, women of the Goddess
If you make a conscious choice
When the North wind blows,
When the ice breaks up in Spring,
When the whip-poor-will sings,
You can smell Me when the lavender blooms.

Or bury your nose in an Artemesia
Rub yourself with marigold petals,
Make love to yourself unashamed,
Wander in a field at harvest, sense
My presence
When you are pacing around outside
When you are upset and furious,
Telling yourself the sad story again.

When you hear crows laughing at you, that's Me
Reminding you, mysteriously
Of course, you already know
If you really need a favor, meet Me
At the crossroads in the dark
Of the Moon, listen for the hounds.

Drop your fear; they won't really tear you apart, surrender
To the greatest good, and I will gift you
With a drop of wisdom for your growing store.

YOU DO NOT HAVE TO BE

You do not have to be what you are not.
What you are is more than sufficient.
It is a whole truth, individual
As a pebble or a shell. Chips and cracks
The odd and awkward growth— those discolorations
Only add to your value.
You don't have to try and be what you are not!
You come from Divine Mystery
With your own destiny, your own
Gifts, ready to hum to those around you,
Fully ready to love— in that particular
Body/soul you were given.
You do not have to try to be what you are not.
Lay down the burden of opinion and expectation.
Wrap your arms around you, feel blood singing
In your arteries, sing your own song.
Listen... give thanks. Walk into the future
With your arms wide open, with your mind
Wide open.

ECLIPSE

It was back before we named ourselves
witches, wild women who sure enough felt we
had to be near water. Water and trees, no
city lights to spoil our lunar eclipse.
We brought a midnight feast, bread, cheese,
fruit and wine and heavy quilts,
while our boyfriends and husbands stayed
home with beer and ballgames.

We adored the sky and Lady Moon eclipsing.
She took her time rising and we passed the evening
with drums and chant, jokes and women's laughter.
Some bared their breasts, after all the lake park was legally
closed; we didn't expect guests.

Some of us danced as Moon began to rise,
insects started a chorus, a barred owl called— and she had owlets!
She would say, plain as day: "Who cooks for you?"
Then a chorus of smaller voices, trying, failing to get it right.
She called again, finally her mate answered far off.
The baby owls went silent, then tried again.

Coyotes howled then and we all traded laughing and lolling
for howling and hooting, churring, letting
go of modern life.

THE YOUNG

Poignant in their awkward beauty
So ignorant that they are followed
By angels... thinking they know the score
How to be hot, or cool, or bored
How to go to the head of the class
"Are they looking at my ass?"
Hearts shattering easily
Like broken mirror glass
Then picking up the pieces
Bouncing back again.
So very interested in the forbidden
But catch them in the act, they will say
They were only kidding.
Living on their machines
Lost in the culture's crazy dreams
Innocent at heart, so eager
To start, to really start!

UNTITLED

When you reach the bottom
A real lifetime low
So mean and dark and slow
You're sure you've had it—
Look around for a light
Even a sparkle will do, a birthday
Candle lit with your last match.
Now look closely at that bottom
And see what you can see
Is there potential to be free?
You did not choose this fate, you're sure
But if not you, then who?
Is there a door, a locked door in the gloom?
Perhaps there's a broom, a hammer
A heavy stone... you've never been so alone
But you know what to do
Dig deeper in reality than you have ever done
Find the shining truth hidden somewhere in the room.

YOU CAN'T GO BACK

You can't go back; the past is gone
The future a shaky branch eager to leaf out
Or possibly break— all you have
Is the Now of now... tentative, alive, breathing.
You can't go back to where you were
That person is gone, a memory.

The question is always who are you
Right now? Does light shine through you?
Is your consciousness contained in your brain?
Is it also in that lizard, that sky, the leaf mold underfoot?
Are you pierced through in this holy moment?

Once again you have the choice
To be more or less than you were,
The choice to embrace your divinity
So that time passing is just one dimension
In the infinite sea of possibility.
You can't go back, a blessing really;
You are free now, and you can go!

HOMAGE TO W. S. MERWIN

'I have to let it open its wings, and fly among the gifts of the unknown.'
I cannot name it or contain it, yet it carries me
Through the undivided universe
Neither in the body or out of it, the wings fluttering
A forgotten swift language of reality, glimpsed through curtains
Of indigo dreams, flying toward the soul knowledge
That dances in every galaxy, every incarnation.
I have to let that burden that I call the self
Be released to these gifts that fly towards me, as
Visions are glimpsed over night deserts
Then disappear, like the luminous eye of deer.
I have to let that great force of love
Open my chakras, past pain and desire
To be reborn into grateful acknowledgment
Dance of infinite energies of possibility
Unfolding on the atomic stages of time
Matter, darkness, stars and sentience, and that shining
Those brilliant wings that fly our hearts past every obstacle
And allow us to sing.

UNTITLED

Never forget your roots are here
You are the corn maiden
The goddess of spring
The green life force made flesh
You walk in your sullen beauty
Like a young queen
Unaware of your elemental power
Trailing a dangerous aura
Of flowers, anger
And half-conscious desire
Men quicken, helpless in your wake
As your girl body
Takes its woman form.

Your world journeys are beginning
The prairie your launching pad
Your roots will keep you strong,
Transplant well
You will give and take nourishment
Wherever you roam
Your foremothers are standing behind you
Their serious and sturdy hands
Gesture from old photographs
Willing you the strength
To endure your long, personal unknown.

IN THE IMAGE OF GOD

Because the ancient arrogant armies that worshiped proud sky-gods
Swept down on the peace-loving people of the great Mother
And tried to destroy her worship
Because Jehovah was a man-god who started right away
Making Eve less than Adam, then punishing everyone
For her natural curiosity
Because Jesus was another male savior, and his mother
Mainly honored for her freaky act of virgin birth
Because Allah was male, and his followers see women
In a rather dim light
And even the historical Buddha had sexist rules for female nuns
Held it difficult to attain enlightenment in a female body
Because the myths were changed, and the rules were changed
Women's power so feared we were vandalized,
Trivialized, and excluded from the halls of power
Because those that loved the earth and celebrated her rhythms
Were burned as witches, while the cosmic dance of male and female
Tipped ever farther from sanity and balance
This is why I sing.

I sing for the Great Goddess, who is not forgotten anymore
And for every creature; I sing for the Earth
Which is fair, I think, as any heaven
Unless we make it our own hell.
I sing for the ones who know light is meaningless
When there is no darkness – the ones that embrace their shadows
Walk their own paths, for those who love their own gender
Or all genders, the guilt-free masturbators and the solitary celibates.

This is for those who risk their lives for a species or ecosystem
And for those who embrace simplicity, and do not need the TV culture
This song is for women, and it is for me.
I reclaim my woman's body and I name it, honor it, part by part.
I praise my eyes that see everything, my kissing lips and restless
 tongue
I thank my clever hands and patient feet, and I say to you: my breasts
 are good.
My nipples are fountains of pleasure for the nursing babe or for the
 lover.

I praise my big belly and the sacred art of Belly Dance
I say my vulva is the holy gateway of life itself.
The delicious intensity of the clitoris belongs to no one except me
I say I am whole, entire, and I do not apologize for the space I take up.
This is my body, a sacred mystery.
I, too, am made in the image of God.

LETTER TO WILDERNESS

Dear wilderness, you steadily
Dwindling resource
Precious beyond worth
And full of Earth's mystery
What will you allow me to see?
I come to you in all seasons
Even a tiny remnant of woods
Is enough, a river
Or a hill. I come to you quietly in
Bitter winter, speak with your bare trees
And what's beyond them
I sense the Mother's energy there
Feel the immanence of spirit
In these earthly bodies— trees, animals
Dry grass murmuring its subtle song.
Dear wilderness, home of all fairy tales
What will you allow me to dream? Fireflies
In black midsummer woods
Beckon me to wander down a path
With no flashlight, humming softly
To the prairie... will you show me the plant divas?
Will the shrine to Mary, deep in the woods
At Shanti Vanam
Glow with her own light
As she once did, as I kneeled in shaking wonder.
Wilderness that is my soul
Will you reveal yourself to me
Even though I'm frightened
Of your wild animals.
If I help you survive
In my little ways
If I pray for you always
Will you agree to stay, and grow
And heal this madly tilting world?

THE LANDSCAPE OF TIME

The landscape of time
Curls through space
At its own pace,
Sometimes dark for ages
With times of light
That strike the psyche
Like lightning
Revealing everything
The elevations, plateaus,
The rivers of blood
Then disappearing into caverns
Or urban taverns where people tope
Oblivious!

The landscape of time
Marks our sad or healthy bodies,
With wrinkles, scars, thinning hair, sagging guts.
It illumines the wisdom we have managed together
Shining from eyes of experience.

The landscape of time
Has no known end, no destination, no special meanings.
Lives come and go, landscapes evolve or devolve
As mountains crumble and rivers
Carve out space!
It is unknowable in essence
Yet we can sense it in the falling leaves,
The cold wind of winter coming in.

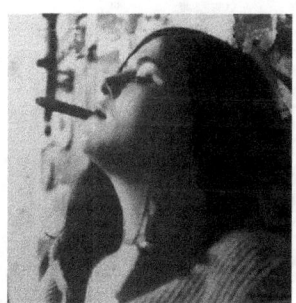

Dixie Lubin is a long-time resident of Lawrence, Kansas, and has been writing for pleasure since she learned to read. She is the author of *Slightly Tilting Towards the Void* (2008) and has had poems published in several anthologies, including *The Carbon Chronicle – Harvest of the Arts Poets* 1992-1996 (Flatland Press), *Begin Again – 150 Kansas Poems* (Woodley Press, 2011), *To the Stars through Difficulties – A Kansas Renga in 150 Voices* (Mammoth Publications, 2012), and *Flash Poems* (Anamcara Press LLC, 2018). Dixie has facilitated community writing workshops, classes, and written with incarcerated teens. She is an outsider artist and a founding mother of the annual Bizarre Bazaar in Lawrence.